# THE TEMPORAL ADMINISTRATION OF THE RELIGIOUS HOUSE OF A NON-EXEMPT, CLERICAL, PONTIFICAL INSTITUTE

This dissertation was approved by Rev. Romaeus O'Brien, O. Carm., J.C.D., as director, and by Rev. John McGrath, A.B., LL.B., J.C.D., and Rev. Frederick McManus, J.C.D., as readers.

THE CATHOLIC UNIVERSITY OF AMERICA
CANON LAW STUDIES
No. 396

# THE TEMPORAL ADMINISTRATION OF THE RELIGIOUS HOUSE OF A NON-EXEMPT, CLERICAL, PONTIFICAL INSTITUTE

A DISSERTATION

SUBMITTED TO THE FACULTY OF THE SCHOOL OF CANON LAW OF THE CATHOLIC UNIVERSITY OF AMERICA IN PARTIAL FULFILLMENT OF THE REQUIREMENTS FOR THE DEGREE OF DOCTOR OF CANON LAW

BY

REV. FRANCIS L. DEMERS, O.M.I., A.B., J.C.L.
PRIEST OF SAINT JOHN THE BAPTIST PROVINCE
OF THE CONGREGATION OF THE OBLATES OF MARY IMMACULATE

THE CATHOLIC UNIVERSITY OF AMERICA PRESS
WASHINGTON, D. C.
1961

IMPRIMI POTEST

Alfred Pelletier, O.M.I.
*Superior Provincialis*

Lowell, Mass., die 2 Februarii, 1961

NIHIL OBSTAT

Frederick R. McManus, J.C.D.
*Censor Deputatus*

IMPRIMATUR

Richard J. Cushing, D.D.
*Archiepiscopus Bostoniensis*

Bostonii, die 14 Februarii, 1961



Printed By
Goulet Printing Company, Nashua, N. H.

TO MY BELOVED

MOTHER

BROTHERS

AND

SISTERS

# FOREWORD

The temporal goods of religious houses are the principal material means of subsistence of religious communities. To assure that the enterprises of such institutes flourish, the Code of Canon Law has laid down various prescriptions that every administrator of religious property must faithfully fulfill. This legislation has been the subject of much study in the past and continues to be the object of research. Nevertheless, many difficulties have yet to be resolved.

The following dissertation is an attempt to throw additional light on some of them. In pursuing this end, the writer has made an effort to take a positive approach to certain problems and to offer some solutions, but it is hoped that his efforts will not be interpreted as an uncompromising attitude towards the opinions of others.

This dissertation confines itself to a study of the general laws of the Church which deals with the temporal administration of local religious houses in non-exempt, clerical, congregations of pontifical approval. Evidently, much of what is written herein is applicable to the administration of temporal goods of every religious institute. But the writer has attempted to deal chiefly with the problems that a local superior of a non-exempt, clerical, institute of pontifical approval may encounter during the exercise of his duty as administrator of the temporal goods that have been entrusted to his care.

Chapter I has been devoted to a study of the historical development of the laws of the Church on the administration of religious property. Chapter II concerns itself with certain concepts concerning the religious house, its right to own property and the limitations of this right. The authority of the local superior in his function as administrator of the temporal goods of a local house has been made the subject of Chapter III. The relationship of the local superior with his treasurer is treated in Chapter IV. Chapters V and VI are devoted to a study of the rights that major superiors and ecclesiastical authorities outside the religious community may exercise over the temporalities of a religious house in non-exempt, clerical, institutes of pontifical approval.

The writer wishes to express his gratitude to his Provincial, the Very Reverend Ferdinand Richard, O.M.I., for the opportunity to pursue advanced studies in Canon Law; to the Faculty of the School of Canon Law of the Catholic University of America for their generous co-operation, and finally, to those who have assisted the writer in any way in the course of this work.

# TABLE OF CONTENTS

TABLE OF CONTENTS (Continued)

# PART II

## Canonical Commentary

TABLE OF CONTENTS (Continued)

# PART I
## Historical Conspectus

# CHAPTER I

## The Evolution of the Temporal Administration of Religious Houses

## INTRODUCTION

The history of the temporal administration of religious houses begins in the early days of monasticism. As a result of the persecutions under such Roman Emperors as Decius (249-251), Valerius (258-260) and especially Diocletian (303-311), a great number of the faithful, particularly in Egypt, withdrew to the deserts. It was then that saint Paul, the anchorite of the Thebaid (341), and saint Anthony (356) started their lives as hermits.

In the beginning, these pioneer religious lived by themselves, isolated from the Christian community.[1] They retired to secluded areas in order to find the solitude necessary for a contemplative life, and each hermit lived isolated from his fellows. Obviously, such a way of life was not without its disadvantages. The hermit could easily fall sick and so need the help of others who would provide what he alone was unable to obtain for himself. It soon became evident that a better plan was for them to unite in groups and live the common life. Such were the circumstances that led to the foundation of the first religious community.

Saint Pachomius (290-346), the father of religious life, founded the first Christian monastery on the shores of the Nile near Tabennisi in the year 330.[2] Later, he founded nine monasteries for men and two for women, and grouped them into the first monastic congregation. Pachomius was its first superior general and visited each house of his small congregation at least once a year. The local superiors also met him twice yearly to discuss financial matters.[3]

---

[1] McManus, *The Administration of Temporal Goods in a Religious Institute,* The Catholic University of America Canon Law Studies, n. 109 (Washington, D. C.: The Catholic University of America Press, 1939), p. 8.

[2] Butler, *The Lausiac History of Palladius* (2 vols., Cambridge, 1898), II, 206.

[3] Kurtscheid, *Historia Juris Canonici, Historia Institutorum ab Ecclesiae Fundatione usque ad Gratianum* (Romae: Officium Libri Catholici, 1951),

The foundation of a monastery appeared to be an advanced stage in the development of monastic life. Ordinarily, a few individuals would group around one monk, remarkable for his holiness, and become his disciples, striving to follow in his footsteps towards their common goal, sanctity of life. This life in common was the starting point of the progressive formation of an institution that was subsequently granted juridical status.[4]

Originally, it was considered that the monastic life should be embraced only by lay people. Consequently the members, like the rest of the faithful, were entirely subject to the local bishop. They had no intention of entering the clerical state, since the sacerdotal life did not seem to be in harmony with their vocation. Monastic life was embraced to pursue one's personal sanctification, a pursuit which seemed irreconcilable with that of the clerical life, since the cleric was ordained for the sanctification of others. Eventually, however, priests and clerics were permitted to enter the monasteries and certain monks were chosen by the religious superior and presented to the bishop for ordination.[5]

Since these groups of lay people emerged from the spontaneous zeal of the faithful and were not created by the Church Herself, no ecclesiastical legislation concerning the administration of monasteries was enacted in the early days of monasticism. The subsequent laws of the Church concerned an institution already existing.

### ARTICLE 1. FROM THE ORIGINS OF MONASTICISM TO ST. GREGORY THE GREAT

Originally, the monasteries enjoyed no juridical status whatsoever. They were merely private associations whose relationships with the

---

p. 181 (hereinafter cited as *Historia Juris Canonici*).

[4] Granic, "L'Acte de fondation d'un monastère dans les provinces grecques du Bas-empire au Ve et VIe siècle" — *Mélanges Charles Diehl* (2 vols., Paris: Librairie Ernest Leroux, 1930), I, 101.

[5] Fournier, *Nouvelle Recherches sur les Curies, Chapitres et Universités de L'Ancienne France* (Paris: Edouard Fournier, 1942), p. 8 (hereinafter cited as *Nouvelles Recherches*): Butler, *Sancti Benedicti Regula Monasteriorum* (2 ed., Friburgi Brisgoviae, 1927), cc. 60-62.

Church and the State were not determined juridically.[6] Until the council of Chalcedon (451), the monasteries remained private institutions and as such were subject only to Roman law in respect to questions of ownership and of administration. Under this law, they were granted the right of property as early as the beginning of the fifth century. In an imperial constitution of 434, found in the Code of Theodosius, it was stated that the monastery could inherit the property of its members who died intestate.[7]

From their very beginning, the majority of monasteries enjoyed a certain amount of wealth, especially those which owed their founding to a benefactor.[8] This prosperity was due primarily to the generosity of the founders, either the king, bishops or pious laymen, who provided the land and defrayed the expenses of the buildings and often left a liberal endowment for the upkeep of the institution.[9] Furthermore, the monks were considered by society as mediators between God and men and for this reason often received generous gifts.[10]

A third source of income was the personal belongings of the monks themselves. The earliest monks ordinarily distributed their property to the poor before entering a monastery. However, they soon realized that the religious community, composed of men who had made the vow of poverty, could become the beneficiary of these goods. There-

---

[6] A l'origine, les monastères se trouvaient en dehors de toute emprise juridique. C'étaient des associations privées d'une espèce à part, dont la situation et les relations n'étaient pas juridiquement déterminées ni vis-à-vis de l'Eglise ni vis-à-vis de l'Empire romain."—Granic, *art, cit.—Mélanges Charles Diehl,* I, 101.

[7] "Si . . . monachus . . . nullo condito testamento decesserit nec ei parentes utriusque sexus vel liberi vel si qui agnationis cognationisve jure junguntur vel uxor extiterit, bona, quae ad eum pertinuerint . . . monasterio, cui fuerat destinatus, omnifariam socientur."—Codex Theodosianus, V, 3, 1; Cf. also Codex Justinianus, I, 3, 20; McLaughlin, *Les Très Ancien Droit Monastique de l'Occident* (Paris, Picard, 1935), p. 204.

[8] Lesne, *Histoire de la Propriété Ecclésiastique en France* (6 vols., Lille; *Faculté, Catholique,* 1910-1943), I, 113.

[9] *Ibid.*

[10] McLaughlin, *Le Très Ancien Droit Monastique,* p. 37.

fore, the aspirant who wished to enter a monastery could leave his earthly belongings either to the poor in the surrounding areas or give them to the monastery he was about to enter.[11] Saint Césaire (470-542) proposed this option to his candidates but they were not bound in any way to follow it.[12] Saint Benedict (529) was the first to direct his monks to give to the monastery the goods remaining to them at the time of their admission.[13] Pope Gregory the Great (590-604) approved this rule of Saint Benedict and made it obligatory for all candidates to religious life.[14] By his religious profession, the monk renounced all property that he might acquire in the future and promised to be satisfied with the clothes and food provided for him by the abbot.[15] Such property relinquished by the monks constituted a fair source of income for the monastery.

The wealth of monasteries was also increased by certain individual property owners who ceded their land to the monasteries but retained the usufruct. By such an arrangement, they enjoyed immunity and certain other privileges granted to the monasteries by the civil authorities.[16] Similar donations were made with the stipulation that the benefactor receive a pension, either in money or in food or clothes for a definite length of time.[17]

---

[11] McLaughlin, *op. cit.* p. 35.

[12] Migne, *Patrologiae Cursus Completus, Series Latina* (221 vols., Parisiis: 1844-1864), LXVII, 1108 (hereinafter cited as *MPL*).

[13] "Res si quis habet, aut eroget pauperibus, aut facta solemniter donatione conferat monasterio, nihil sibi reservans ex omnibus."—Butler, *Sancti Benedicti Regula Monasteriorum*, p. 109.

[14] Quia ingredientibus monasterium convertendi gratia ulterius nulla sit testandi licentia, sed res eorum ejusdem monasterii juris fiant, aperta legis definitione decretum est."—*Gregorii I Papae Registrum Epistolarum—Monumenta Germaniae Historica*, Epistolarum Tom. I and II (ediderunt P. Ewald et L. Hartmann, Berolini, 1891-1899), Ep. IX, 197 (hereinafter cited as *MGH, Registrum Epistolarum*).

[15] " . . . quippe qui ex illo die nec proprii corporis potestatem se habiturum scit."—Butler, *op. cit.*, p. 109.

[16] Poupardin, *Recueil des Chartres de Saint-Germain-des-Prés* (2 vols., Paris, 1909), I, 13.

[17] For a detailed study of this question, cf. Lesne, "Une source de la fortune monastique: Les donations à charge de pension."—*Mélanges de Philosophie et d'Histoire de la Faculté des Lettres de l'Université Catholique de Lille* (Lille: 1927), 33-47.

As the number and size of the monasteries increased, their influence upon the surrounding population became more pronounced. From time to time, they interfered in ecclesiastical affairs, making it expedient for the Church to determine their exact juridical status. Accordingly, in the ecumenical council of Chalcedon (451), the Church settled the problem and determined the juridical status of the monasteries in the Church. This council expressly required the approbation of the local bishop for the foundation of a monastery within his territory and subjected the monasteries to his jurisdiction. At the same time, this council officially recognized the monasteries as moral persons and conferred upon them juridical personality. This legislation enabled them to enjoy the same rights and privileges as other similar institutions in the Church such as parishes and dioces.[18] Finally, the council decreed that the monks were to be subject to the local bishop and that the bishop was to exercise a strict but benevolent vigilance over the religious communities within his territory.

The Fathers of the council were aware of the evils that had been inflicted at times on the monasteries by unscrupulous men, often the very ones who were entrusted with their care. The monasteries had grown in wealth and had often become the envy of men who wishes

---

[18] "Qui vere et pure solitariam eligunt vitam, digni sunt convenienti honore. Quia tamen quidem monachi habitu utentes, res communes disturbant, indifferenter civitates circumeuntes, necnon et monasteria per se ipsos propria prasumptione constituere tentant; placuit, neminem aut aedificare aut constituere monasteria, aut oratorii domum, sine conscientia ipsius civitatis episcopi. Eos vero, qui per singulas civitates seu possessiones in monasteriis sunt, subjectos esse debere episcopo, et quieti operam dare atque observare jejunia et orationes, in locis in quibus semel Deo se devoverunt, permanentes; et neque communicare ecclesiasticis, neque saeculares aliquas tractare actiones, relinquentes propria monasteria, nisi forte jubeantur, propter urgentes necessitates, ab ipsius civitatis episcopo. Et neminem servorum suscipi in monasterium, ut sit cum eis monachus nisi cum domini proprii conscientia. Praetereuntem vero haec decrevimus extra communionem esse, ne nomen domini blasphemetur. Convenit vero civitatis episcopo, curam solicitudinemque necessariam monasteriis exhibere."—Council of Chalcedon, c. 4—Harduin, *Acta Conciliorum et Epistolae Decretales ac Constitutiones Summorum Pontificum* (12 vols., Parisiis, 1715), II, 601 (hereinafter cited as Harduin).

to enrich themselves at their expense. To put an end to various conflicts that had arisen, the council, in its twenty-fourth canon, required that the monasteries remain moral persons in perpetuity and that their property be not secularized. Those who permitted such actions to take place were to be subjected to canonical penalties.[19]

As a result of this legislation, monasteries enjoyed the right to own property and to administer their temporal goods. As moral persons approved by the Church, they obtained certain fundamental rights which could be exercised only by lawfully empowered officials who acted in the name of the monastery. Their goods could be administered only by those legally empowered to do so. The monastery, as the legal owner of its property, enjoyed a certain independence and immunity from the jurisdiction of the local prelate in the administration of its property. Although the foundation of a monastery depended on the permission of the bishop, once it had been founded, its capacity to administer property was independent of his authority. This was not a question of exemption from episcopal jurisdiction but an application of fundamental rights of moral persons. The particular law of each monastic order stated clearly that the abbot was the administrator of the property of the monastery and that the collectivity of the monks was absorbed in his person.[20]

The majority of prelates seemed to have recognized this relative independence of monasteries in temporal affairs. Unfortunately, a few prelates claimed the right to administer the temporalities of the monasteries within their territory and to make regulations concerning the internal regimen of the monastic communities. They managed to inject themselves into the administration of these communities, giving as reasons both the protection of the foundation and the jurisdiction that they enjoyed over all Christians within their diocese.

This failure to acknowledge the independence of monasteries in the administration of their property gave rise to serious difficulties.

---

[19] "Quae Deo semel sacrata sunt monasteria secundum episcopum consensum, oportet in perpetuum monasteria nuncupari, et eorum res monasteriis reservari, et non debere ulterius coenacula saecularia fieri." C. of Chalcedon, c. 24—Mansi, *Sacrorum Conciliorum Nova et Amplissima Collectio* (53 vols., in 60, Paris, 1901-1927), VII, 399 (hereinafter cited as Mansi).

[20] McLaughlin, *op. cit.*, p. 44.

Later councils attempted to bring a solution to this problem by defining the exact relationships between the abbot of the newly-formed monasteries and the hierarchy of the Church.[21] However, some prelates, little disposed to see the monasteries within their territories enjoy complete autonomy in the administration of their property, in accordance with their constitutions, still attempted to control and limit the powers of the abbot. For example, in the canons of the French councils may be found decrees stating that the abbot could not alienate any property of the monastery without the authorization of the bishop.[22] The third council of Orleans (538) stipulated in canon 23 that the abbot might not sell objects that had been destined to divine cult without the same authorization.[23] Three years later, in 541, the fourth council of Orleans, reiterating the legislation of previous councils, decreed that gifts donated to a monastery did not belong to the abbot. Moreover, the council renewed the obligation of the abbot to obtain the permission of the bishop for all acts of alienation.[24]

The third council of Orleans had also permitted the local bishop to entrust the administration of the monasteries within his territory to a diocesan priest of his choice.[25] Acting under this decree, the

21 Kurtscheid, *Historia Juris Canonici*, p. 315.

22 "In venditionibus, quas abbates facere presumunt, hec forma servetur, ut quicquid sine episcopi licentia venditum fuerit ad potestatem episcopi revocetur." Council of Agatha, c. 56—c. 40, C. XVII, q. 4.

23 "Abbatibus . . . de rebus ecclesiasticis, vel sacro ministerio, alienare vel obligare absque permissu et subscriptione episcopi suit nil liceat. Quod qui praesumpserit, regradetur communione concessa, et quod temere praesumptum aut alienatum est, ordinatione episcopi revocetur."—Mansi, IX, 18.

24 "Si quid abbatibus, aut sacris monasteriis, aut parochiis pro Dei fuerit contemplatione collatum, in sua proprietate hoc abbates vel presbyteri minime revocabunt; nec alienare quod cunctis fratribus debetur quacumque occasione praesumant. Quibus si fuerit necessarium ut statuta convellant, non aliter valeat, nisi fuerit episcopi sui subscriptione firmatum."—Mansi, IX, 115.

25 "De his vero clericorum personis, quae de civitatensis ecclesiae officio monasteria, dioeceses, vel basilicas in quibuscumque locis positas, id est sive in territoriis, sive in ipsis civitatibus suscipiunt ordinandas, in potestate sit episcopi, si de eo quod ante de ecclesiastico munere habebant, eos aliquid aut nihil exinde habere voluerit: quia unicuique facultas suscepti monasterii, dioecesis, vel basilicae, debet plena ratione sufficere." III Council of Orleans, c. 18—Mansi, IX, 18.

bishop of Clermont in France entrusted to a priest of his choice the administration of the monastery of Chantoin, situated near the episcopal See.[26] The monastery of Holy Cross in the diocese of Poitiers was administered by the local bishop in the same manner as the parishes of the diocese.[27] Some prelates even seized the property of monasteries; some took advantage of the opportunity offered by the vacancy of the abbatial office on the death of the abbot to alienate the monastic patrimony. This practice was condemned by the council of Paris held in 614 and was considered as contrary to the general feeling of the French episcopacy.[28]

However, the independence of monasteries concerning the administration of their property was acknowledged by the majority of councils. During the third council of Arles (455) a certain hostility arose between the abbot of Lerins and the bishop of Marseille, and thus provided an occasion to determine the rights of both the prelate and the abbot. The bishop claimed certain rights over the monks who had not received sacred orders. The council declared that the bishop of Marseille enjoyed jurisdiction only over those monks who had received holy orders and to that extent only, and that the monks who had not entered the clerical state were under the exclusive jurisdiction of the abbot.[29] This decision of the council strongly indicates that the jurisdiction of the local prelate did not extend to

---

26 McLaughlin, *op. cit.*, p. 46, note 2.

27 "Et ei (the bishop of Poitiers) hoc monasterium sicut reliquas parochias, regulariter liceat gubernare." This text is cited in McLaughlin, *op. cit.*, p. 46, n. 2.

28 "Comperimus denique, cupiditatis instinctu, deficiente abbate, presbytero, vel his qui per titulos deserviunt, praefidium quodcumquo in mortis tempore dereliquerint, ab episcopo vel archidiacono diripi, et quasi sub augmentum ecclesiae vel episcopi, in usum ecclesiae revocari, et ecclesiam Dei per pravae cupiditates expoliatam relinqui. Statuimus observandum, ut neque episcopus, aut archidiaconus exinde aliquid auferre praesumat: sed in loco ubi moriens hoc dereliquerit, perpetualiter debeat permanere." Council of Paris, c. 8—Mansi, X, 541.

29 Monasterii vero omnis laica multitudo ad curam abbatis pertineat: neque ex ea sibi episcopus quidquam vindicet, aut aliquem ex illa clericum, nisi abbate petente, praesumat . . . laica vero omnis monasterii congregatio ad solam ac liberam abbatis proprii, quem sibi ipsa elegerit, ordinationem, dispositionemque pertineat; regula, quae a fundatore ipsius monasterii dudum constituta est, in omnibus custodita." III Council of Arles—Mansi, VII, 908; Lesne, *Histoire de la Propriété Ecclésiastique en France,* I, 126; Sirmond, *Concilia Antiqua Galliae,* (3 vols., Paris, 1629), I, 121.

temporal matters, and that the administration of the property of the monastery was entrusted to the abbot.[30]

The disciplinary measures decreed by the council of Arles are also found in African legislation. At the synod of Carthage (525), an important decision was reached on the problem of temporal administration. An abbot named Peter, whose monastery had been unduly burdened by the local bishop, appeared before the synod and pleaded for exemption from the jurisdiction of the prelate concerning temporal matters. He gave as reason that his monastery had been built by the members of the order and had not been founded nor endowed by the prelate.[31] In response to this request, the synod decreed that all monasteries were to be freed of the obligations incumbent on the diocesan clergy.[32]

A few years later, the council of Carthage (534) confirmed the decree of the synod of 525. In regard to the decision rendered by the synod concerning the monastery of the abbot Peter, the council maintained that the monasteries must enjoy the highest degree of freedom consistent with the legislation of the previous councils and that, in financial matters, they be entirely independent of the bishops and in no way indebted to them.[33]

---

[30] Concerning this decree of the council of Arles, Thomassinus writes: "Ex hac ergo Synodali Constitutione emicat, potestatem temporalem penes unum fuisse Abbatem: et quoad spiritalem, obnoxium fuisse Episcopo monasterium tum quod nisi ejus nutu et arbitrio haberi non posset Ordinatio, Chrisma, Confirmatio, tum quod nec extranei admitti possent, nisi eo annuente Clerici. Caeteroquin omnia administrabat Abbas vel jure communi, vel consensione certissima Episcopi, quae in jus communi evasisset."—Thomasinus, *Vetus et Nova Ecclesiae Disciplina circa Beneficia et Beneficiarios* (10 vols., Moguntiac, 1787), Pars I, lib. III, cap. 26, n. 16 (hereinafter cited as *Vetus et Nova Disciplina*): " . . . on est en droit de déduire que l'évèque ne s'occupe en rien du temporal."—Fournier, *Nouvelles Recherches,* p. 10.

[31] "Ideoque humiles supplicamus . . . a jugo nos clericorum, quod neque nobis neque patribus nostris, quisquam superponere aliquando tentavi, eruere digneris."—Mansi, VIII, 653.

[32] "Erunt igitur omnia omnino monasteria sicut semper fuerunt, a conditione clericorum modis omnibus libera, sibi tantum et Deo placentia."—Mansi, VIII, 656.

[33] "Au sujet du monastère de l'abbé Pierre, dont l'abbé est maintenant Fortunat, il faut s'en tenir aux décisions du concile tenu sous Boniface. Les autres monastères doivent également jouir de la plus grande liberté, autant que le permettent les conciles . . . Pour tout le reste, les monastères sont indépendents de lur évêque, et ne lui doivent aucune redevance."—Héfélé-Leclercq, *Histoire des Conciles,* II, 2a pars, p. 1138-1139.

This same trend prevailed in Spain where the influence of African legislation in this matter seemed to have been felt. The council of Lerida (584) decreed that the temporalities donated to a monastery were in no way subject to the diocesan laws promulgated by the bishop.[34]

In summation, from the foundation of the first monastery to the pontificate of Saint Gregory (590-604), the legislation of various councils acknowledged the right of monasteries to own property and the constitutions of every monastic order entrusted the administration of this property to the abbot. The exercise of these rights, however, was restricted by various prelates who wanted to consider monasterial property on an equal plane with parochial property. Such pretentions gave rise to the conflicts which characterized much of this period. Pope Saint Gregory the Great, however, soon ended the conflict by clearly defining the jurisdiction of the local bishop over the monasteries within his territory.

## ARTICLE 2. FROM GREGORY THE GREAT TO THE COUNCIL OF TRENT

The credit of inculcating respect for the autonomy of the monks in temporal administration belongs to *Pope Gregory the Great* (590-604).[35] In his numerous letters to bishops throughout Christendom, Pope Gregory stressed again and again the principle that monasteries be independent of the local prelate in regard to temporal matters. These official papal pronouncements finally abated the conflict between monks and prelates and served to bring them to a greater degree of cooperation with each other.

Evidently, Pope Gregory recognized the power of the bishop in regard to certain aspects of monastic life. To indicate this power, he

---

34 " . . . ea vero quae in jure monasterii de facultatibus offeruntur, in nullo diocesana lege ab episcopis contingantur."—Council of Lerida, c. 3—*MPL*, LXXXIV, 323.

35 Kurtscheid, *Historia Juris Canonici*, p. 317; Fournier, *Nouvelles Recherches*, p. 13; McManus, *The Administration of Temporal Goods in Religious Institutes*, p. 54; McLaughlin *Le Très Ancien Droit Monastique de l'Occident*, pp. 46-47.

often used the terms: *diligentia disciplinae,*[36] *cura*[37] and *cura dispositioneque.* [38] The term most often used, however, is *jurisdictio.*[39] Since the bishop was responsible, above all others, for the faithful observance of monastic life, this jurisdiction entailed the right and the duty of vigilance over the monasteries,[40] the right to visit the monasteries in order to inspect the foundations and ascertain that the will of the benefactors and of the founders was faithfully observed.[41]

This jurisdiction, however, did not entail the right to interfere in the administration of monastic property. On this subject, Pope Gregory was very clear and his principles never wavered.[42]

At the beginning of his pontificate, in 592, Pope Gregory wrote a letter to Castor, Bishop of Armenia, stating that the bishop might not exercise any power whatsoever in monasteries without the permission of the abbot and that the monks must always remain under

---

36 "Ita ut in eodem monasterio neque fraternitas tua neque presbyteri praeter diligentiam disciplinae aliquid molestarium inferat aut si quid pro diversorum devotione commoditatis accesserit sibi aestimet vendicandum."—*MGH, Registrum Epistolarum,* Ep. III, 58.

37 "Oportet ergo ut fraternitas tua erga monasteria civitatis parochiaeque suae omnes subjectos pastorali cura diligenter invigilet et de vita actuque eorum sit omnino sollicitata"—*MGH, Registrum Epistolarum,* Ep. VI, 11.

38 "Monasteria . . . sub tua cura dispositioneque."—*MGH, Registrum Epistolarum,* Ep. VI, 21.

39 "Tantummodo sit jure contento et monasterium illud nulli alterius alii quam generali canonicaeve jurisdictioni deserviens remotis vexationibus ac cunctis gravaminibus . . . "*MGH, Registrum Epistolarum,* Ep. V, 49.

40 "Sed ille eorum vitam competenti regularique debet moderatione disponere, qui pro comissis eorum sibi animabus compellitur reddere rationem."—*MGH, Registrum Epistolarum,* Ep. IX, 203.

41 Cf. *MGH, Registrum Epistolarum,* Ep. VIII, 17.

42 "Mais c'est surtout à l'égard de la propriété monastique que le pape légiféra le plus souvent pour arrêter les prétentions de l'épiscopat. Sur ce point, le programme de Grégoire est très net et ne varie jamais."—McLaughlin, *Le Très Ancien Droit Monastique,* p. 151.

the authority of their abbot, so as to avoid misunderstandings between the bishop and the monks.[43]

Again, in a letter addressed to a sub-deacon named Gratiosus, the Pope mentioned that due consideration must be given to those who had chosen the religious life. He ordered Gratiosus to grant certain property-rights to a local group of religious in order to preserve peace in the Church.[44]

In 595, Saint Gregory wrote to Marinianus, bishop of Ravenna, asking him not to revoke the privileges already granted by his predecessor to a monastery in his territory, and requesting that the present order of things be kept intact.[45]

During the same year, he wrote another letter to bishop Castor in answer to complaints lodged in Rome by abbot Luminosus. The abbot of the monastery of Saint Andrew and Thomas had notified

---

43 "Luminoso abbate referente plurimis in monasteriis multa a praesulibus praejudicia atque gravamina monachos pertulisse cognovimus. Oportet ergo, ut tuae fraternitatis provisio de futura quiete eorum salubri disponat ordinatione . . . Nec audeat ibi episcopus cathedram collocare, vel quamlibet potestatem exercere imperandi, nec aliquam ordinationem, quamvis levissimam, faciendi, nisi ab abbate fuerit rogatus, quatinus monachi semper maneant in abbatum suorum potestate, ut remotis vexationibus a cunctis gravaminibus divinum opus cum summa devotione animi perficiant."—c. 6, C.XVIII, q. 2.

44 Religiosan vitam eligentibus nos oportet congrua consideratione prospicere, ne cujusdam necessitatis occasio aut desides faciat, aut robur (quod absit) conversationis infringat. Idcirco praesenti tibi auctoritate praecipimus, quatinus domum positam in hac urbe, regione quarta, juxta locum, qui appellatur gallinas albas, vel ortum juris sanctae Romanae, cui auctore Deo presidemus ecclesiae, in qua Campana quondam Patricii mansisse dinoscitur, simul et ortum atque hospitia, que intra eandem domum janua conclusit, eidem debeas tradere proprietatis jure proculdubio possidendam, in qua domo monasterium ubi cum congregatione sua habitare possit, Christo adjuvante construere, et tam ipsa quam que in ejus honore locoque successerit predictam domum et ortum cum omnibus ad se pertinentibus (sicut diximus) quieto et inconcusso jure a nobis pietatis consideratione concessam valeat possidere."—c. 75, C. XII, q. 2; Jaffé, *Regesta Pontificum Romanorum* (2 ed., 2 vols., Lipsiae, 1885-1888), I, 1221 (857) (hereinafter cited as Jaffé).

45 " . . . adhortandam, ut nihil de his, que illic contulit atque constituit, aliquo modo patiatur inminui, sed omnia firma stabilitate studeat servari."—c. 3, C. XII, q. 5; Jaffé, 1380 (1011).

the Holy See of certain abuses practiced by the bishop. Saint Gregory consequently notified bishop Castor that, at the death of the abbot, he was not to disturb, in any way whatsoever, the administration of the patrimony of the monastery.[46]

In another letter to Marinianus, in 598, Saint Gregory reaffirmed that bishops must not interfere in the temporal administration of monasteries. Relying on his supreme authority as successor of Saint Peter, he explicitly forbade bishops or lay people to claim any revenue whatsoever from monastic property, or to change or jeopardize the economic condition of monasteries.[47]

It must also be mentioned that Gregory reasserted the principle of freedom of access to Rome and of correspondence with Rome. For any motive useful to the monastery, the abbot could appeal to the Roman Pontiff and present his case to him in order to safeguard the rights of the monastery.[48] Thomassinus mentioned that Pope Gregory asked the bishop of Marseilles to abstain from interferring in the administration of the monastery of Saint Cassien.[49]

The preceding quotations from the letters of Pope Gregory indicate clearly that, according to him, the monasteries must be autonomous in regards to their temporal administration. Until the pontificate of Saint Gregory, the jurisdiction of the local bishops over

---

46 "Luminosus abbas monasterii sanctorum Andreae et Thomae, in Ariminensi civitate constituti, quas nobis lacrymabiliter preces effuderit, inditae textus petitionis informat. Pro qua re fraternitatem tuam hortamur, ut, obeunte abbate monasterii ipsius, Ecclesia tua in describendis providendisque acquisitis acquirendisve ejusdem monasterii rebus nulla se occasione permisceat."—*MPL,* LXXVII 578; Jaffé, 1362 (997).

47 "Quam sit necessarium monasteriorum quieti prospicere . . . Interdicimus igitur in nomine Domini nostri, ex auctoritate B. Petri apostolorum principis . . . ut episcoporum nullus aut saecularium ultra praesumat de redditibus, vel cartis monasteriorum, vel de cellis vel villis, quae ad ea pertinent, quocumque modo seu qualibet occasione minuere, vel dolos vel immissiones aliquas facere."—c. 5, C. XVIII, q. 2.

48 "Quotiens autem pro utilitate monasterii sui ad Romanum Pontificem abbas venire vel transmittere forte voluerit, ei modis omnibus liceat."—*MPL,* LXXVII, 919; Jaffé, 1504 (1138).

49 "Ut nec Episcopus, nec ejus clericorum quisquam ullam partem attingeret administrationis temporalium." — Thomassinus, *Vetus et Nova Disciplina,* Pars, I, lib. III, cap. 30, n. 1.

monasteries had never been clearly determined. Everyone admitted that the monks were subjected to their ordinary, but this principle had never been put into practice. The council of Chalcedon, stipulated that monks be subject to their bishop, but such a statement did not grant unlimited powers to the prelate. On the other hand, although the monks enjoyed a certain independence in regard to their internal affairs, the limits of such an autonomy had never been defined. Saint Gregory, a monk himself, put an end to all doubts in that matter. He declared that the administration of the monastery be in the care of the abbot; but he also wished that in spiritual matters such institutions should be guided by the Bishop of the diocese. The two great principles of his program were the recognition of the jurisdiction and disciplinary powers of the bishop over the monasteries and the acknowledgment of the independence of monasteries in the administration of their temporalities.[50]

After the pontificate of saint Gregory, the number of papal documents concerning monastic life decreased surprisingly. However, the few documents that have reached us indicate that the legislation of Pope Gregory had paved the way for the privilege of exemption.

The first document of importance is a bull of Pope Honorius (625-638) addressed in 628 to Bertulf, abbot of a Norman monastery in Bobbio founded by saint Columban. In his request, the abbot asked that his monastery be placed under the jurisdiction of the Holy See and that it be submitted to no one else.[51] The pope granted the request of Hertulf and forbade the local bishop to exercise any jurisdiction whatsoever over the monastery.[52] This exemption was the

---

[50] "Jurisdiction et pouvoir disciplinaire de l'évêque sur le monastère et libre administration du monastère par la communauté, voilà les grands traits du programme pontifical sur cette question si épineuse à toutes les époques."—McLaughlin, *Le Très Ancien Droit Monastique,* p. 183.

[51] "Petis nec igitur, ut monasterium . . . privilegia sedis apostolicae largiremur, quatenus sub juridictione sanctae nostrae . . . ecclesiae, constitum nullius ecclesiae juridictionibus submittatur, pro qua re piis votis facilites (faventes) (h) ac nostra auctoritate, id quod a tua dilectione exposuimus (exposcimur) effectui mancipari (mancipamus)." This text is cited by McLaughlin, *Le Très Ancien Droit Monastique,* p. 187, note (2).

[52] "Et ideo, omnem cujuslibet ecclesiae sacerdotem in praedicto monasterio dicionem qualibet auctoritate ne extendere (auctoritatemve extendere) atque sue auctoritate nisi a praeposito monasterii fuerit invitatus, missarum solemnitates celebrare omnino prohibemus." This text is cited by McLaughlin, *Le Très Ancien Droit Monastique,* p. 187, note (3).

first of a vast current that followed[53] and was largely due to the influence of Irish monks. These monks enjoyed complete exemption from episcopal authority in their own land, and through their extensive travels on the continent fostered the idea of monastic independence. The Norman monastery of Bobbio was an example of such an establishment, where Celtic principles exercised a great influence upon Church legislation. Since this monastery was a powerful center of Catholic doctrine and a stronghold against the Arian heresy, it was granted a very broad degree of exemption, much broader than ordinarily conceded.[54]

The Holy See granted complete exemption to an ever-increasing number of monasteries. The basic reason for this procedure is to be found in the canons of the earlier councils and in the letters of Pope Gregory the Great, which stated the principle that exemption of the monasteries from episcopal jurisdiction in internal affairs was a "matter of right and justice".[55]

The burning problem during the period immediately following the pontificate of Gregory the Great was that of the rights of lay founders of monasteries in regard to the temporal goods of their foundation. The existence of a monastery was often due to the initiative of a wealthy lay land-owner who opened a haven of prayer on his

---

[53] Kurtscheid, *Historia Juris Canonici*, p. 317; McLaughlin, *Le Très Ancien Droit Monastique*, p. 188; Creusen, *De Juridica Status Religiosi Evolutione* (Apud Aedes Pont. Univ. Gregorianae, 1948), p. 20; Zeiger, *Historia Juris Canonici* (2 vols., Romae, Apud Aedes Universitatis Gregorianae, 1939), II, 89. One author upheld that the first exemption was granted in 509, on the 21st of August to Saint Vincent Monastery of the Order of Saint Benedict: cf. Tamburini, *De Jure Abbatum et Aliorum Praelatorum* (4 vols., Coloniae Agrippinae: 1691), disp. V, a. XI. n. 10. However, this exemption was granted by the bishop of Paris and not by the Roman Pontiff.

[54] "Bobbio était le centre d'une vie religieuse intense en Lombarbie, pays devenu la proie de l'hérésie arienne. Afin d'établir un rempart contre les ariens, de garder un foyer lumineux de doctrine catholique et de s'assurer de la fidélité et de l'orthodoxie constante de ce monastère, le pape a voulu lui accorder une liberté plus étendue, en le rattachant au siège romain. La place brillante que Bobbio occupa par la suite démontre bien la sagesse de cette mesure si libérale."—McLaughlin, *Le Très Ancien Droit Monastique*, p. 188.

[55] McManus, *The Administration of Temporal Goods in Religious Institutes*, p. 65.

property. He provided the members of the institution with the daily necessities drawn from his own wealth. Consequently, he retained a high degree of interest in the foundation and because of his generosity to the monastery, he claimed the right to administer its temporalities.[56] Such rights were also claimed by lay owners of monasteries, who had acquired the monasteries either by inheritance or by way of gift.[57]

Foremost in the ranks of lay founders and owners of monasteries were the kings, to whose generosity many monastaries, especially in France, owed their origin. Saint Medard at Soissons, Saint Germain des Prés of Paris and Saint Denis in the Province of France were examples of such monasteries. From the fifth century, in Italy, the kings appropriated some monasteries and gave them gratuitously to their officers or even to their courtesans. In vain did the popes and the bishops object to this practice. This license continued in France until the reign of Dagobert (600-659), who favored the Church more than did his predecessors. Unfortunately, the practice was revived by Charles Martel (689-741).[58]

During the reign of Pepin, the council of Ver (755) discussed the problem and in its twentieth canon prescribed what was to be done with the money and goods given to a monastery for the upkeep of the monks. It also required that the abbot render an account of his administration to the bishop if the monastery was controlled by the bishop and to the king if it was controlled by the king.[59]

Besides the king, other lay persons founded and owned monasteries, and reserved to themselves the *dominium* over the goods that they had contributed.[60] According to the juridical ideas of the times, they were empowered to guarantee or at least to supervise the administration of the endowment. It is quite evident that the builder

---

[56] Fournier, *Nouvelles Recherches*, p. 22.

[57] McLaughlin, *Le Très Ancien Droit Monastique*, pp. 238-243.

[58] Fournier, *Nouvelles Recherches*, p. 63.

[59] "In alia synodo nobis perdonastis, ut illa monasteria, ubi regulariter monachi vel monachae vixerunt, hoc quod eis de illis rebus dimittebatis unde vivere potuissent, exinde, si regalis erat, ad domnum regem faciant rationes abbas vel abbatissa; et si episcopalis, ad illum episcopum. "Council of Ver. c. 20—Mansi, XII, 584.

[60] Creusen, *De Juridica Status Religiosi Evolutione*, pp. 24-33.

and founder of a monastery enjoyed definite rights both over the temporal goods of the monastery and the persons of the monastery.[61]

Since such conditions were detrimental to monastic life and security, a reform became imperative.[62] The Sovereign Pontiffs reacted against these abuses by granting exemptions to numerous monasteries, subjecting them to the jurisdiction of the Holy See, so that the monasteries were subject only to the Roman Pontiff even in regard to the administration of their temporal goods.[63]

Local ordinaries and also particular councils legislated against these abuses. In 940, Rathier, bishop of Verona, reminded civil authorities of the preeminence of the authority of the abbot, who, in all things pertaining to his stewardship, was not to be limited by the temporal authorities. According to Rathier, the king is the guardian of the Church but not her administrator . . . her patron but not her minister.[64] The council of Bourges (1031) commented on the principle established by the bishop of Verona in its twenty-first canon and stated that no lay person could receive a benefit from a monastery.[65] The council of Toulouse (1056) also concerned itself with this question and prohibited lay persons from interfering with the government of monasteries.[66]

Indults granting exemption from all lay influence in the monasteries became more and more numerous. Innocent II (1130-1143) granted two-hundred and eighty indults; Eugene III (1145-1153) granted three-hundred and ninety-seven; Alexander III (1159-1181) granted six hundred and thirty-five.[67] Slowly, the will of the

---

61 McLaughlin, *Le Très Ancien Droit Monastique*, pp. 243-245; Kurtscheid, *Historia Juris Canonici*, p. 315.

62 Kurtscheid, *op. cit.*, p. 316.

63 Kurtscheid, *Historia Juris Canonici*, p. 316.

64 *MPL*, CXXXVI, 284.

65 Mansi, XIX, 505.

66 "Quia audivimus quosdam laicorum, nefario ausu, res ecclesiasticas suis usibus applicuisse, et injuste dominio, in suum opus, retinuisse omnimodis prohibemus; ut nemo laicorum abbatiam monachorum, vel clericorum, archidiaconatum neque preposituram, vel honorem presbyterii, vel Sacristae, seu magistri scolae, neque ullos honores, ad jus predictum pertinentes, ausit suis usibus retinere, et si fecerit excommunicationi subjaceat."—Mansi, XIX, 848.

67 Kurtscheid, *Historia Juris Canonici*, p. 316, note (2).

Sovereign Pontiffs and of local ecclesiastical authorities prevailed. The rights of lay persons over the property of monasteries decreased and the authority of the abbot over the monastic property became independent of all lay influence.

Before the legislation of the council of Trent concerning the administration of monastic property may be studied, mention must be made of the abbeys *in commendam.* Ever since the pontificate of Gregory the Great, (590-603), some monasteries had been asked by the Holy See to grant benefices to certain diocesan priests who were in no way bound by the rules of the monastery nor subject to the abbot.[68] The abbey was therefore in these instances compelled to give a part of its revenues to one who was not a member of the community. In return, there was no compensation granted to the abbey. This stranger was often named abbot of the monastery and even permitted to assume the role of administrator of the monastery.[69]

From the seventh to the twelfth century, the concession of such privileges to members of the secular clergy was not too frequent.[70] The number multiplied however during the twelfth and thirteenth centuries so that more and more monasteries became thus burdened. This increase may be easily explained. During this period of Church history, the Holy Land had fallen into the hands of the Saracens, and, as a consequence, many bishops were expelled from their dioceses and deprived of their regular income. Naturally, they turned to the West in search of means of livelihood. Although the Sovereign Pontiff hoped in time to restore the exiles to their Sees, he had, meanwhile, to assure their maintenance. Consequently, he assigned them to monasteries which provided the temporal necessities through a share in the revenues of the monastery.

---

68 Laprat, "Commendes"—*Dictionnaire de Droit Canonique* (5 vols., Paris: Letouzey, 1955- ), III, 1029 (hereinafter cited as *DDC*).

69 "In plurimis monasteriis Abbates vel priores a Sancta Sede, a regibus, ab episcopis nominabantur, quibus monasterium 'commendabatur'; saepe non erant monachi et de bonis monasterii sibi vidicandis unice solliciti erant." Creusen, *De Juridica Status Religiosi Evolutione*, pp. 29-31.

70 Laprat, "Commendes"—*DDC*, III, 1030.

This provisional arrangement was indeed a boon to the exiled bishops. It was accepted by the monks, however, with some reluctance, though they were powerless to remedy their situation, particularly since in some instances, the prebendaries had been granted by the Holy See.[71] Neither the Church nor the State seems to have fought energetically against the situation. Chapters and Councils legislated only against the more serious abuses. As a result, the practice continued to expand and by the fourteenth century, it was considered quite normal.[72] Although Pope John XXII (1313-1334) increased the actual number of these prebendaries, he did endeavor to suppress the plurality of these benefices in his noted constitution *Exsecrabilis*.[73] On the other hand, Pope Benedict XII (1334-1342) made serious efforts to abolish this practice altogether. In 1335, he revoked all privileges of this kind granted by Pope John XXII, with the exception of those conferred upon the cardinals, an exception made at the request of Cardinal Orsini.[74] A few years later, Pope Innocent VI (1352-1362) took similar measures.[75] His meager success, however, indicated how deeply entrenched this custom had become. Often, one Pope would suppress this practice during his pontificate, only to have his successor reinstate it.[76]

The council of Constance (1417), in its first decree, stated that the incoming Pope should introduce reform in the Church, particularly in the matter of prebendaries. Other reform projects initiated by the council requested the revocation of all privileges of this kind.[77]

Another effort in this direction was that of Pope Martin V (1417-1431) who suspended the privileges granted to prelates, even to cardinals, over monasteries and priories numbering more than ten religious.[78] The last attempt to correct this situation, before the

---

71 Van Espen, *Jus Ecclesiasticum Universum* (5 vols., Louvain: 1778), I, 323.

72 *DDC*. III, 1031-1032.

73 C. un., *de preabendis et dignitatibus*, III, in *Extravag. Joann XXII.*

74 Laprat, "Commendes"—*DDC*, III, 1050.

75 *Ibid.*

76 *Ibid.*

77 Mansi, XXVII, 1164; Laprat, "Commendes"—*DDC*, II, 1951.

78 Héfélé-Leclercq, *Histoire des Conciles*, VII, 2a pars, 496.

whole matter was brought up for consideration by the council of Trent, was made by Pope Leo X (1513-1521) in his famous bull *Supernae Dispositionis* of May 5, 1514. Therein, he stipulated that heretofore vacant monasteries should not be granted as prebendaries and that they should be administered by persons fulfilling the conditions required by law.[79]

In summary, theoretically, the freedom of monasteries in the administration of their temporal goods was recognized as the law of the Church from the sixth century until the Council of Trent. In practice, however, the exercise of this right was often restricted by the greed of certain individuals. But, there were exceptions to the general rule. In certain cases, the abbot was obliged to render an account of the administration either to the founder, to a civil officer, or to the bishop, if the laws of the foundation so decreed.[80] Goods entrusted to the religious, but destined for a parish or for pious work were subject to the supervision of the local Ordinary as were the execution of pious wills and testaments.[81]

---

[79] *Bullarium Taurinum*, V, 605-606. Fundamentally, these decrees changed nothing in the actual state of affairs. A great number of such privileges were still granted and consequently, the law was rendered ineffective. Cf. Laprat, "Commendes"—*DDC*, III, 1057.

[80] Cf. p. 18.

[81] "In Lateranensi concilio noscitur fuisse prohibitum, ne quilibet regulares ecclesias seu decimas sine episcoporum consensu de manu laici praesumant accipere . . . Nos autem id fortius inhibentes, transgressores digna curavimus animadversione punire, statuentes nihilominus, quatenus in ecclesiis, quae ad ipsos pleno jure non pertinent, juxta ejusdem concilii statuta episcopis instituendos presbyteros repraesentent, ut illis de plebis cura exhibeant competentem, institutos vero removere non audeant episcopis inconsultis."—c. 31, X, *de praebendis et dignit.*, III, 5;
. . . tam religiosi quam clerici saeculares et laici, pecuniam et alia bona quae per manus eorum ex testamentis decedentium debent in usus pios expendi, non dubitant aliis usibus applicari. Quum igitur in omnibus piis voluntatibus sit per locorum episcopos providendum, ut secundum defuncti voluntatem universa precedant, licet etiam a testatoribus id contingeret interdici." c. 17, X, *de test. et ult. vol.*, III, 26. "Religiosis, etiam exemptis, deputatis ad exsecutionem cujuslibet ultimae voluntatis, circa ipsius exsecutionis officium . . . volentes praescindere materiam delinquendi, praesentis constitutionis auctoritate statuimus, quod tales, etiamsi praelationis fungantur officio, locorum ordinariis debitam reddere, ipsique ordinarii ab eisdem absque dolo, fraude seu negligentia de susceptae exsecutionis officio teneantur exigere rationem, illae quos circa id deliquisse repererint, in aliorum exemplum poena debita, quocunque non obstante privilegio, punituri."—c. un., *de test et ult. vol.*, III, 6, in Clem.

## ARTICLE 3. FROM THE COUNCIL OF TRENT TO THE CODE OF CANON LAW

### *Section I. The Council of Trent*

The Council of Trent considered the administration of the temporal goods of religious houses in its twenty-fifth session. It granted to monasteries the right to acquire property unless exception was made in specific cases.[82]

One of the decrees of this session stated that the administration of temporal goods of a religious house should be conducted by a bursar or an econome: "The administration of the property of monasteries or convents shall belong to the officials thereof only, who are removable at the will of their Superiors.[83]

Moreover, the council was aware of the plight of the monasteries held *in commendam* and recognized the impossibility of applying the measure to monasteries whose revenues had been given to persons outside the control of the monasteries themselves. Most of these monasteries had suffered great losses, spiritual as well as temporal, through the maladministration of those to whom they had been entrusted. The council wished therefore to restore them entirely to a discipline consonant with monastic life. But the actual state of affairs was so full of difficulties that a remedy could not be applied to all monasteries at once, nor could a common remedy be applied everywhere. Nevertheless, the council provided that professed re-

---

82 "The holy Council grants that all monasteries and houses of men as well as of women, and of mendicants, even those that were forbidden by their constitutions or that had not received permission to this effect by Apostolic privilege, with the exception of the houses of the brethren of St. Francis, the Capuchins and those called Minor Observants, may in the future possess immovable property. But if any of the foresaid places, to which it has been granted by Apostolic authority to possess such property, have been deprived thereof, it decrees that the same shall be wholly restored to them." Sess. XXV, *de regularibus,* c. 3—Schroeder, *Canons and Decrees of the Council of Trent* (St. Louis: Herder, 1941), p. 219.

83 Sess. XXV, *de regularibus,* c. 2—Schroeder, *Canons and Decrees of the Council of Trent,* p. 218.

ligious of the institute be placed over monasteries which were then held *in commendam.* It furthermore stipulated that vacant monasteries should in the future be entrusted to religious of the institute who were recognized for their virtue and holiness. The beneficiaries of the more important monasteries were either to resign or to make solemn profession of the vows of the particular order within six months. Otherwise, monasteries held *in commendam* were to be considered *ipso jure* vacant. The council entrusted the execution of its canon to the Holy Father who was to enforce it as he saw fit.[84]

Unfortunately, this attempt of the council to suppress the concessions did not meet with complete success. The Italian prelates, it seems, had been opposed to the suppression.[85] Moreover, the interpretation of the canon itself gave rise to different opinions. It was questioned whether the prohibition contained in the canon

---

[84] "Since such monasteries, also abbeys, priories and provostries, have suffered no little loss in spiritual and temporal things through the maladministration of those to whom they have been entrusted, the holy council desires to restore them entirely to a discipline becoming the monastic life. But the present state of the times is so adverse and so full of difficulties that a remedy cannot be applied to all at once or a common one everywhere. Nevertheless, that it may not omit anything that may in time provide advantageously for the aforesaid, it trusts in the first place that the most holy Roman pontiff will according to his piety and prudence make it his care, so far as he sees the times will permit, that regulars expressly professed in the same order and capable of guiding and governing the flock be placed over those monasteries which are now held *in commendam* and which have their own convents. Those which in the future become vacant shall be conferred only on regulars of approved virtues and holiness. With regard to those monasteries which are the head and chief ones of the orders, whether their filiations be called abbeys or priories, they who now hold them *in commendam* shall be bound, if a regular has not been appointed as successor thereto, to make within six months a solemn profession of the vows peculiar to those orders or to resign; otherwise the aforesaid places shall be considered *ipso jure* vacant. But that in each and all of the aforesaid matters no fraud may be perpetrated, the holy council decrees that in the appointments to the monasteries mentioned, the character of each person be expressly stated, and any appointment made otherwise shall be considered surreptitious and shall not be protected by any subsequent possession, even though this covers a period of three years." Sess. XXV, *de regularibus,* c. 21—Schroeder, *Canons and Decrees of the Council of Trent,* pp. 230-231.

[85] Laprat, "Commendes"—*DDC,* III, 1064.

applied to primatial abbeys alone or to all monasteries and convents of every order. The Congregation of the Council decided that only the primatial abbeys were subject to the canon and that inferior convents could be granted *in commendam* to members of the secular clergy or to lay persons. On the other hand, the Auditors of the Sacred Rota interpreted the text of the council as proscribing the concession of *any* convent to anyone but to a member of the regular clergy.[86] Whatever may have been the divergence of opinion on the matter, the first opinion prevailed in practice. The Roman Pontiffs themselves entrusted various Benedictine and Cistercian monasteries to members of the secular clergy. The primatial abbeys of these two orders, however, were never subject to such concessions.[87]

### *Section II. Monasteries of Women*

Before considering the administration of temporal goods in institutes with simple vows, something should be said of the administration of temporal goods in monasteries of religious women. Some of

---

86 "Cap. 21, sess. 25 de regular. caveatur ut monasteriis, quae tunc commendata reperiebantur, et suos Conventus habebant, Regulares personae ejusdem ordinis expresse professe praeficerentur; quae vero in posterum vacabunt non nisi regularibus conferantur: et Domini de Rota intellexerint ea verba praeceptive, non consultive, et hunc dixerint esse sensum perfectum, ne de cetero alicui non regulari conferantur . . . tamen oppositum declaravit sacra Congregatio Cardinalium ejusdem Concilii Interpretum: nam proposito dubio, an Concilium d.c. 21 censeatur praecipere ne detur de commenda in commendam: censuit non censeri, cum utatur verbo illo, *confidit,* quot verbum comprehendit etiam illum vers. *quae vero.* Et quando Concilium vult praecipere, utitur in frequentibus verbo *teneantur.*"—Fagnanus, *Commentaria in Quinque Libros Decretalium* (5 vols., Coloniae Allobragum: 1759), t. I, 2a pars, p. 87.

87 "Et hinc collige notabilem limitationem ad conclusionem proxime firmatam, qua dictum est Concilium non prohibere quin beneficia regularia saecularibus commendentur, ut non procedat quoad monasteria, quae sunt Capita Ordinum: nam de his Concilium per verba praeceptiva, seu obligatoria in eod. c. 21 . . . Qua ratione forsitan factum est, ut Romani Pontifices, qui pleraque monasteria S. Benedicti, et Cistertiensis Ordinis dederunt in commendam saecularibus Clericis: tamen non commendaverint monasterium Cassinense, quod est Caput illius Congregationis nec monasterium Cisterti, quod est Caput Ordinis Cistertiensis."—Fagnanus, *op. cit.,* p. 87; cf. also Van Espen, *Jus Ecclesiasticum Universum* (5 vols., Louvain: 1178), t. I, p. 324.

these monasteries also enjoyed the privilege of exemption whereby they were subject only to the Holy See. However, since the Holy See could not supervise all of them, the Council of Trent ordered them to group themselves into congregations which would be governed by general chapters.[88] While this change was in process, the individual convents were to be under the jurisdiction of the local Ordinary who was to fill the role of a delegate of the Holy See.[89]

Notwithstanding the desires of the Council, the traditional customs unfortunately remained. The monasteries continued to claim exemption from the local Ordinary and since the Holy See was unable to control the entire administration, the abuses persisted. Lay persons continued to interfere with the administration of the monasteries, and to appropriate the revenues. For their part, the bishops endeavored to make use of their delegated powers and to administer the monasteries according to the wishes of the Council but they met with little success.[90]

Pope Gregory XV (1621-1623) attempted to remedy these abuses. He extended the law submitting religious women to the local Ordinary and decreed that all monasteries of religious women, even those subject to the regular clergy, should thereafter be subject to the local Ordinary in all matters both temporal and spiritual. He compelled the administrators of monasteries to make an annual report to the

---

[88] "All monasteries which are not subject to general chapters or to bishops, and which have no regular visitors who belong to the order, but have been accustomed to be governed under the immediate protection and direction of the Apostolic See, shall be bound within a year from the dissolution of the present council and thereafter every three years, to assemble in congregations in accordance with the form of the constitution of Innocent III published in the general council, which begins '*In singulis*' and they shall there authorize certain regulars who shall deliberate and decide on the manner and order of establishing the aforesaid congregations and also the rules to be therein observed." Sess. XXV, *de regularibus*, c. 8—Schroeder, *Canons and Decrees of the Council of Trent*, pp. 222-223.

[89] Sess. XXV, *de regularibus*, c. 9—Schroeder, *Canons and Decrees of the Council of Trent*, p. 223.

[90] S. C. Ep. et Reg., Spalatin, 9 March 1593—*Codicis Juris Canonici Fontes* (Cura Emi Petri Card. Gasparri editi, 9 vols., Romae: postea Civitate Vaticana: Typis Polyglottis Vaticanis, 1923-1939), (Vols. VII-IX, ed. cura et studio Emi Justiani Card. Seredi), n. 1478 (hereinafter cited as *Fontes*).

bishops concerning their administration or become liable to penalty. The local Ordinary was empowered to ask the superiors to remove certain administrators. If he received no cooperation, he could remove the administrators himself when he deemed it necessary.[91]

The regulations of Gregory XV for the administration of temporal goods in convents of women became permanent law. The succeeding Popes confirmed this legislation.[92] However, not every female religious order submitted immediately to this legislation. Indeed Pope Benedict XVI (1740-1748) admitted that the pontifical sanctions were neither observed nor executed.[93]

## *Section III. Administration in Congregations with Simple Vows*

### A. Before the Apostolic Constitution *Conditae a Christo*

Before the sixteenth century, no simple-vow institute had been chartered by Rome. Institutes with solemn vows alone were recognized. Moreover, the foundation of new orders was explicitly forbidden. Anyone wishing to become a religious had to join one of the existing and approved orders, and anyone establishing a new monastery, was obliged to adopt a rule of life already approved by the Holy See.[94] During the sixteenth century, however, contrary to

---

91 "Sed et administrantes bona ad eadem Monasteria Sanctimonialium, ut praefertur, etiam regularibus subjectarum, pertinentia, sive regulares exstiterint, sive saeculares, quomodolibet exempti, Episcopo loci, adhibitis etiam superioribus regularibus, singulis annis rationes administrationis, gratis tamen exigendas, reddere teneantur, ad idque juris remediis cogi, et compelli queant." Gregory XV, const. *Inscrutabili,* 5 Feb., 1622—*Fontes,* n. 199.

92 "Nos igitur . . . ad exactam, et plenariam Constitutionum memoratorum Gregorii, et Clementis Praedecessorum observationem, prout eos concernunt, omnino teneri, et obligates existere . . . statuimus et declaramus." Clement XII, const., *Admonet nos,* 11 Aug. 1735—*Fontes* n. 297.

93 " . . . eadem Pontificum sanctiones usu minime receptas esse, neque executioni unquam demandatas, uti plurium annorum experientia cognovimus." *Institutiones Ecclesiasticae* Prosperi Lambertini S.R.E. Cardinalis Archiepiscopi Bononiensis, postea Benedicti Decimi Quarti Pont. Opt. Max.; (Romae: Typis Sacrae Congregationis De Propaganda Fide, 1747), p. 135.

94 "Ne quis de coetero novam religionem inveniat, sed quicumque ad religionem converti voluerit unam de approbatis assumat."
IV Lateran Council (1215), c. 13—c. 9, X, *de religiosis domnibus,* III, 36.

the legislation of the fourth Council of Lateran, many communities arose whose members professed simple vows.[95] As a result in 1521, Pope Leo X (1513-1521) suppressed such Institutes as had been erected without the permission of the Holy See.[96] On November 17, 1568, Pope Saint Pius V (1566-1572), in his constitution *Lubricum vitae genus,* ordered superiors of male institutes wherein the common life was followed without solemn vows, to ask their subjects to declare within twenty-four hours whether or not they wished to pronounce solemn vows. Those who answered negatively were required to withdraw from the institute, and the others were granted a month during which they were to decide which set of Rules they would approve or accept.[97] The prescriptions of this constitution, however, were apparently not strictly enforced, and the law fell into desuetude by reason of the foundation of numerous congregations of simple vows.

During the seventeenth century, few of these congregations were approved.[98] In 1623, Saint Vincent de Paul (1581-1660) founded the congregation of the Mission. Although Pope Urban VIII (1623-1644) approved the institute, the vows that its members pronounced were not received by the Church as public vows. Other congregations similar in nature were founded in the course of time. Since the vows professed in these institutes, however, were not public, these congregations were not considered as religious institutes in the strict sense of the word.

During the eighteenth century, the number of approbations increased. Benedict XIV (1740-1758) was the first Pope to initiate legislation concerning congregations with simple vows, in his constitution *Quamvis Justo,* dated April 30, 1749.[99]

---

[95] Sipos, *Enchiridion Juris Canonici* (Rome: Herder, 1954), p. 270.

[96] Leo X. const. *Inter Coetera,* 20 Jan. 1521—*Magnum Bullarium Romanum* (8 vols., Luxemburgi: 1727), I, 616.

[97] Pius V. Const. *Lubricum vitae genus,* 17 Nov., 1568—*Bullarium Diplomatum et Privilegioum Romanorum Pontificum Taurinensis Editio* (24 vols., et Appendix, Augustae Taurinorum, 1857-1872), III, 147 (hereinafter cited as *Bull. Rom. Taur.*).

[98] Creusen, *De Juridica Status Religiosi Evolutione,* p. 36.

[99] *Fontes,* II, n. 398.

During this period, no ecclesiastical legislation can be found directly concerning the administration of temporal goods in these institutes.[100] The founders drew up sets of rules and of constitutions which the members followed and these constitutions contained regulations concerning the administration of the temporalities. However, these constitutions could be changed by the General Chapter or by the Ordinaries. Thus the laws varied greatly according to the institute. Therefore, no uniform legislation can be found prior to the promulgation of the constitution *Conditae a Christo* of Leo XIII.

Regarding the matter of religious institutes of women, the members pronounced vows as did the religious members of male institutes, and ordinarily were affiliated with a first Order. In 1521, Pope Leo X (1513-1521) had approved and confirmed the Sisters of the Third Order of Saint Francis as an institute of simple vows.[101] In 1566, however, Pope Saint Pius V (1566-1572) stated clearly in his constitution *Circa Pastoralis* that these institutes were abolished and declared that in the future no Third Order would be recognized unless the members pronounced solemn vows and observed the rule of enclosure.[102]

No further important legislation was enacted until 1816 when Pope Pius VII (1800-1823) approved the constitutions of the Sisters of Charity.[103] Three years later, papal approbation was finally granted to an institute of women with simple vows. Pope Pius VII thus

---

[100] Bastien, *Directoire Canonique* (5 ed., Bruges: Beraert, 1951), p. 22.

[101] "Et quoniam in dicta Tertia Regula quaedam maritatis accomoda, caelibi vero virgineoque statui sub hujusmodi Tertia Regula Domino famulantibus nullatenus decentia innectuntur, ob quod castrorum animorum nitidi affectus ac juxta Domini voluntatem, pretiosum a vili separantes, eamdem Tertiam Regulam in modum qui sequitur distinctam de novo confirmamus et approbamus." Leo X, const. *Inter Coetera,* 20 Jan. 1522—*Magnum Bullarium Romanum,* I, 617.

[102] "Mulieres quoque quae Tertiariae, seu de Poenitientia dicuntur, cujuscumque fuerint Ordinis in congregatione viventes . . . . . . si votum solemne non emiserint, Ordinarii una cum superioribus earum hortentur, et persuadere studeant, ut illud emittant, et profiteantur, ac post emissionem et professionem eidem clausurae se subjiciant." Pius V, const. *Circa Pastoralis,* 29 May, 1566—*Fontes,* n. 112.

[103] *Acta Pii VII,* II, 1227.

paved the way for future approvals and thus abrogated the previous laws forbidding institutes of simple vows.[104] The constitution of Pius VII gave impetus to the formation of many congregations of simple vows, both of men and of women. Some were approved by the Holy See; others received only espiscopal approbation. However, the rights and the obligations of such institutes remained uncertain and controverted.[105] To dispel such doubts, Leo XIII (1873-1903) issued the constitution *Conditae a Christo* on December 8, 1900, a document since called the "Magna Carta" of the religious congregations.[106] With the issuance of this constitution the juridical character of congregations of simple vows, whether of papal or of diocesan approval, was clearly defined for the first time.

B. The Apostolic Constitution *Conditae a Christo*

The purpose of this constitution was to determine the rights of the Ordinaries over diocesan and pontifical congregations. The Pope first gave the division of religious institutes with simple vows: 1) diocesan institutes which owe their existence to the authority of the local Ordinary; and 2) pontifical institutes which have received at least the "decree of praise" from Rome.

The Pope disposed of the administration of temporal goods of diocesan institutes in very few words: *Episcopus . . . jus habet de economicis rationibus cognoscendi*".[107] The Holy Father granted to the bishop the right to supervise the temporal administration of diocesan institutes. This right of supervision evidently did not include the right of direct administration. The local religious superiors of such institutes remained the legal administrators of the houses in accordance with the decrees of the council of Trent.[108] However,

---

104 Pius VII, const. *Dominici Gregis*, 14 Dec. 1819—*Bull. Rom. Taur.*, VII, 1990.

105 McGrath, *The Local Superior in Non-Exempt Clerical Congregations*, The Catholic University of America Canon Law Studies, n. 351 (Washington, D. C.: The Catholic University of America Press, 1954), pp. 12-22.

106 *Fontes*, n. 644.

107 *Conditae a Christo*, ch. I, n. I—*Fontes*, n. 644.

108 Sess. XXV, *de regularibus*, c. 2—Schroeder, *Canons and Decrees of the Council of Trent*, p. 218.

if, in the constitutions approved by him, the local Ordinary reserved to himself certain administrative acts, he could legitimately perform such acts. He could also determine in the constitutions the limits of ordinary and of extraordinary administration. If nothing was determined in the constitutions, the rights of the bishop seem to have been limited exclusively to the right of supervision. Within these limits he could personally inquire into, or be informed by others about, the administration of each local house, and also about the amount of the patrimony. He was empowered to prescribe special norms to be followed by the administrators, and, if the case arose, change the administrators themselves, after having informed the superiors. On the other hand, once the constitutions had been approved and the administrators had been named, he could not determine how the goods were to be used nor reserve to himself the partial or total distribution of the goods of the local houses nor of the institute.

The Pope granted more power to the superiors of pontifical institutes and less to the local Ordinaries. Since these congregations reach into several dioceses, it is only reasonable that the power of local Ordinaries be limited to permit a greater freedom of action to the members of such institutes.[109]

Thus, the Constitution stated: "The rights of distributing official functions . . . belongs to the Chapters and to the Councils proper to each house."[110] In the case of female institutes, the local Ordinary could preside at the chapter, but only as a delegate of the Holy See, and not by virtue of his own authority. Furthermore, the Constitution remained silent on the right of the Ordinary to approve or annul an election in a female institute.[111]

The superior general and his Council were entrusted with the administration of the temporal goods of the institute and each local house was to be administered by the local superior, according to

---

109 "Quia nimirum in dioceses plures propagantur, eodemque ubique jure unoque utuntur regimine; ideo Episcoporum in illas auctoritatem opus est temperationem quandam admittere certosque limites." *Conditae a Christo*, Introduction.

110 *Conditae a Christo*, ch. II, n. 1.

111 *Conditae a Christo*, ch. II, n. 2.

the rules and constitutions.[112] The Ordinary was not allowed to exact an account of the administration. However, if funds had been given or willed to a particular house in order to provide for public worship or for charitable undertakings within the locality, the local superior had the right to administer such funds, but had to make a report to the Ordinary, with perfect deference to his instructions. The superior, man or woman, could not conceal from the Ordinary any part of these funds, neither could he transfer them to other uses. The Ordinary could examine the accounts of funds received or disbursed at any time he wished. He was obliged to ensure that the capital was preserved and the interest not squandered.[113]

The Holy Father also stressed the point that boarding schools, hospitals, schools and asylums conducted by members of pontifical institutes remained under the vigilance of the Ordinary in matters pertaining to religion.[114] Former faculties or privilages granted by the Holy See, or rights acquired by centenary, immemorial custom, or contained in rules and constitutions approved by the Holy See, remained intact. These norms were law for every pontifical institute, including non-clerical institutes.[115]

C. The *Normae* of the Congregation of Bishops and of Regulars.

In 1901, the Congregation of Bishops and of Regulars reiterated in a series of norms the prescriptions of the constitution *Conditae a Christo*. It added, however, that a financial report must be sent to the Holy See every three years.[116] The norms also required that superiors of female institutes submit this report for examination by

---

[112] *Conditae a Christo,* ch. II, no. 9. "Bonorum, quibus Sodalitia singula potiuntur, administratio penes Moderatorem supremum maximamve Antistitam eorumque consilia esse debet: singularum vero familiarum redditus a praesidibus singulis administrari oportet, pro instituti cujusque legibus. De iis nullam Episcopus rationem potest exigere."

[113] *Conditae a Christo,* ch. II, n. 9.

[114] *Conditae a Christo,* ch. II, n. 10.

[115] *Conditae a Christo,* ch. II, n. 11.

[116] *Normae secundum quas S. Cong. Ep. et Reg. procedere solet in approbandis novis institutis votorum simplicium,* 28 June, 1901, n. 262. (hereinafter cited as *Normae* of 1901.)

the local Ordinary of the diocese in which the mother-house is located before sending it to the Holy See.[117] An additional provision required that each house with an annual surplus should remit one third of its net proceeds to the provincial superior and that each province, in turn, remit one-third of its annual surplus to the general superior of the institute.[118]

## D. The Instruction *Inter Ea*

Since the stability and the security of religious communities were endangered by the too great facility with which debts were incurred, the Sacred Congregation of Religious issued, in 1909, an Instruction for religious communities.[119] It forbade religious superiors to contract, in the future, any notable debt, without the previous consent of their council or of higher superiors. It also determined the *meaning* of this notable amount as follows: five hundred to one thousand lire for a local house; one thousand to five thousand lire for a province, and five thousand to ten thousand for the general curia.[120] For all debts in excess of ten thousand lire the administrator was obliged to obtain the *beneplacitum* of the Holy See. These sums marked the limits of the powers of the respective superiors in matters relating to debts.

Interpretation of this article of the instruction varied amongst different authors.[121] First, a number of authors believed that the local superior could not incur a debt over five hundred lire without a special permission. The provincial superior, however, could grant this permission only if the amount was less than a thousand lire. To incur a debt above one thousand lire, the permission of the

---

117 This norm provided the basis for canon 510 of the present Code.

118 *Ibid.*, n. 294.

119 S. C. de Rel., Instruction, *Inter Ea,* 30 July, 1909—*Acta Apostolicae Sedis, Commentarium Officiale* (Romae: (1909 ——), I, 695-699 (hereinafter cited as *AAS).*

120 "In debitis vel obligationibus oeconomicis contrahendis habenda notabilis quantitas, quae superat 500 libellas nec attingit 1,000 si agatur de monasteriis vel domibus singulis . . . Quod si domus . . . debita vel obligationes contrahere intendat, quae valorem 10,000 libellarum excedant, praeter licentiam . . . Concilii, ut supra, requiritur beneplacitum apostolicum." *Inter Ea,* n. II.

121 Besson, *L'Instruction Inter Ea* (Paris: 1912), pp. 26-28.

superior general was necessary. Others were of the opinion that the local superior could incur a debt of five hundred lire, but special permission was required for one amounting to more than five hundred lire but less than a thousand. The consent of the provincial superior was necessary for every debt above the amount of a thousand lire, but in this case, the debts had to be incurred by the Province. A third group of authors believed that debts of notable value for a local house were those between five hundred and a thousand lire. They maintained that the Sacred Congregation only wished to determine an approximate concept of the notable value, by giving the two extremes. Consequently, the authors applied the principle *in dubiis libertas,* until a formal declaration from the Holy See would settle the question. However, no such declaration was issued before the Code.[122]

The Instruction also determined how the different councils, general, provincial and local, were to be founded and conducted, and established the conditions necessary to undertake new constructions. Moreover, it gave rules concerning the administration of mass foundations and of dowries.[123] An institution with rules and constitutions stricter than those contained in the Instruction might follow its own rules. However, an institute whose rules were opposed to the instruction would have to abrogate them. In the final article, the Instruction stated that the preceding prescriptions concerned religious orders as well as religious congregations, and that transgressors would be punished to the full extent of the law.

With the issuance of the Instruction *Inter Ea,* a notable step had been taken toward the formulation of the common law concerning the temporal administration in religious congregations. It remained for the Code to perfect and supplement this previous legislation.

---

122 Besson, *L'Instruction Inter Ea,* p. 8.

123 *Inter Ea,* arts. V, VI, VII, VIII, IX, XI, XII.

# PART II

## Canonical Commentary

# CHAPTER II

## PRELIMINARY QUESTIONS

Before undertaking a commentary on the laws of the Code governing the administration of temporal goods in a religious house of a non-exempt, clerical, pontifical institute, it is necessary to examine certain terms that will be used throughout this dissertation.

### ARTICLE 1. THE ERECTION OF A RELIGIOUS HOUSE

The Code defines a religious house as the house of any religious institute.[1] This is a narrower usage than was accepted before the Code. In pre-Code law, the term was applied to hospitals, orphanages, schools and similar institutions, whether they were blessed, consecrated or destined by ecclesiastical authority for any religious purpose.[2]

The term, religious house, may be considered either in a material or in a formal sense. Taken materially, it applies to the place or building in which the religious live. In its formal connotation, the term designates the religious community; namely, the lawfully erected moral person which constitutes the smallest integral unit in the religious institute.[3] Unless the house has been erected by lawful

---

1 *Codex Juris Canonici Pii X Pontificis Maximi jussu digestus Benedicti Papae XV auctoritate promulgatus, Praefatione, Fontium Annotatione et Indice Analytico-Alphabetico ab Emo Petro Card. Gasparri Auctus* (Romae: Typis Polyglottis Vaticanis, 1917; reimpressio 1948), can. 488, 5°. Hereinafter, reference to this work is made merely by means of the abbreviation "can." for canon, followed by the appropriate number.

2 "Domus religiosae in sensu specifico, seu non sacrae, in quibus citra consecrationem ex authoritate episcopi pietatis, et misericordiae opera exercentur: uti sunt monasteria, collegia, cetraeque domus regularium; item xenodochia, in quibus peregrini, nosocomia, in quibus aegroti; orphanotrophia, in quibus orphani recipiantur, et substentantur, etc. . . "—Schmalzgrueber, *Jus Ecclesiasticum Universum* (12 vols., Rome: Ex Typographia Rev. Can. Apostolicae, 1844), lib. VII, tit. XXXVI, n. 1-4 (hereinafter cited as Schmalzgrueber).

3 Flanagan, *The Canonical Erection of Religious Houses,* The Catholic University of America Canon Law Studies, n. 179 (Washington, D. C.: The Catholic University of America Press, 1943), p. 25.

authority it does not qualify as a religious house, regardless of the number of members dwelling in it. It must also fulfill two conditions: it must have its proper superior; and it must have been lawfully designated as a place for the observance of the religious life.[4] The absence of one or both of these elements excludes certain types of houses; such as, villas, farmhouses and other similar residences used primarily for secular purposes; likewise, residences with no independent legal standing of their own are not religious houses in the proper sense.

If a religious house is erected as a collegiate moral person, at least three members of the religious community must be assigned to it at the moment of its erection.[5] Once the house has been thus erected as a moral person, it remains such, even though the number of religious attached to it should fall below the number required for its erection. The consequent rights and obligations will generally have to be ascertained from particular law. However, if a house is canonically erected as a non-collegiate moral person, the number of religious assigned to the house may be less than three at the moment of its erection; if the number of members is increased, additional rights and obligations may be acquired.[6]

The Code, in canon 488, 5°, refers to three kinds of religious houses; a house of regulars, a formal house and a non-formal house.

---

[4] Pejska, *Jus Canonicum Religiosorum* (3 ed., Friburgi: 1927), p. 49.

[5] Can. 100. § 2; Coronata, *Institutiones Juris Canonici* (5 vols., Vol. I, 4 ed., 1950; Vol. II, 4 ed., 1951; Vol. III, 4 ed., 1956; Vol. IV, 4 ed., 1955; Vol. V, 3 ed., 1951, Rome: Marietti), I, 619 (hereinafter cited as *Institutiones*); Battandier, *Guide Canonique pour les Constitutions des Instituts à Voeux Simples* (6 ed., Paris: 1923), p. 422 (hereinafter cited as *Guide Canonique*); Brisebois, *De Natura Juridica Domus Religiosae* (Rome: Pont. Ath. Ant., 1955), p. 45; Larraona, Commentarium in Partem Secundam libri II Codicis, quae est: "De Religiosis"—*Commentarium pro Religiosis* (Romae: 1920-1934; ab anno 1935: *Commentarium pro Religiosis et Missionariis*, III (1922), 48, note (176) (this article hereafter cited as "Commentarium Codicis" and the periodical as *CpR* and *CpRM* respectively).

[6] Vermeersch, "Quaestiones de Codice Canonico"—*Periodica de Religiosis et Missionariis* (Brugis, 1905-1919; ab anno 1920, *Periodica de Re Canonica et Morali utilia praesertim Religiosis et Missionariis*, Brugis, 1920-1927; ab anno 1927; *Periodica de Re Morali, Canonica, Liturgica*, Brugis, 1927-1936, et Romae, 1937- ), (1922), (34)-(35) (hereinafter cited as *Periodica*).

A house of regulars is defined as the house of an Order whose way of life is based on a Rule (Regula). The Code has no specific term to indicate the house of a congregation. To designate these houses, it employs such terms as the *house of a religious congregation,* a *religious house belonging to a congregation,* or simply, a *religious house.*[7]

A formal house is one in which six professed religious reside. When the house belongs to a clerical institute at least four of the members must be priests. (The Code, in canon 488, 5°, mentions only the minimum number required.) Although six professed religious are required to establish such a house, it is not necessary that every one be perpetually professed.

One cannot argue on the basis of the principle stated in canon 102, § 2 that a formal house remains such when it ceases to have the required number of members through the death or transfer of some of them. The text of the canon clearly states that six religious must actually be assigned to the house. The word *degunt* must be taken in the sense of actual residence in the house in question. If the number of members falls below the number of six, the house will remain a moral person, but will not be considered a formal religious house (domus formata).[8]

A non-formal house, on the other hand, is one that satisfies some, but not all of the requirements of law for a formal house. Either it does not have six religious assigned to it, or, as in the case of a clerical institute, it does not have four priests attached to it, even though six religious may actually be residing there. Regardless of the number of religious assigned to the house, it should be erected canonically if it is to be a permanent residence. Otherwise the members would be living outside a religious house.

Besides the three categories of religious houses mentioned above, a fourth kind of religious house is mentioned in the constitutions of religious institutes; the filial house. *Domus filialis,* in the strict sense, denotes a house which is not juridically independent but is subordin-

---

[7] Cans. 498, 512, § 1, 2°, 604, §§ 1-2.

[8] Larraona, "Commentarium Codicis"—*CpR,* III (1922), 52.

ated to a principal house to which it is attached. Its community is directly subject to the superior of the principal house who is its immediate and proper superior. Such a house, therefore, has no legal existence or moral personality apart from the independent religious house to which it is attached.[9] A filial house, being merely an extension, as it were, of the house to which it is attached, has no canonical superior other than the superior of the principal house,[10] although it may be under the actual supervision of a delegate of the superior. It may happen, however, that the constitutions grant the director of the filial house certain rights proper to the local superiors. These rights will usually concern his relationships with his religious subjects. Moreover, since it is not an independent house, it will not possess property of its own,[11] and the religious assigned to this house will exercise their capitular rights in the chapter of the principal house.[12]

Canonical erection means the concession of moral personality through an act of the competent ecclesiastical authority or by a prescription of law, whereby an association or an institute is recognized as a moral person in the Church.[13] As applied to a religious house, the term denotes the creation of a moral person that pertains to the religious state, in a site where a definite community has permanent residence. This act does not imply the necessity to erect or own a building, since a religious house can be erected in a building already constructed, which does not belong to the religious community.

---

[9] Creusen, "Fondation de Maisons Religieuses"—*Revue des Communautés Religieuses* (Enghien, Belgique: 1929- ), XI (1935), 99 (hereinafter cited as *RCR*); S.C. Rel., Reply, 1 Feb., 1924— Bouscaren, *Canon Law Digest* (4 vols., Milwaukee, Bruce Publishing Co., 1934, 1949, 1953, 1958), I, 278.

[10] S.C. de Rel., Reply, I Feb., 1924—Bouscaren, *Canon Law Digest,* I, 278.

[11] "Quod attinet autem ad *domos stricte filiales,* ex ipso juris communis praescripto eaedem incapaces possidendi habendae sunt, utpote quae propriam communitatem constituere non possint, nec bona propria possidere, sed sint "quasi membra domus majoris, a qua omnimode dependent".—S.C. Rel., Reply I Feb., 1924—Bouscaren, *Canon Law Digest,* I, 278.

[12] Bastien, *Directoire Canonique,* p. 26, n. 42, 5°.

[13] Can. 100, § 1; Larraona, "Commentarium Codicis"—*CpR,* V (1924, 418; Coronata, *Institutiones,* I, p. 619, n. 521; Shaefer, *De Religiosis ad norman Codicis Juris Canonici* (3 ed., Rome: S.A.L.E.R., 1940), p. 153, n. 79 (hereinafter cited as *De Religiosis*).

Several authorities must intervene in the erection of a religious house: the internal authority of the institute; the local Ordinary; and, in some cases specified in canon 497, § 1, the Holy See. Ordinarily, the initial act belongs to the competent religious superior who decides to establish a new house. Since the Code is silent concerning the competent superior for the establishment of a new religious house, the constitutions of the institute will usually determine this question. The *Normae* of 1901 required that, in the case of congregations with simple vows, the superior obtain the consent of the council by means of a deliberative vote before proceeding to the establishment of a new religious house.[14] This requirement has not been included in the new legislation of the Code and therefore may be regarded as no longer in force.

After the competent religious superior has decided to erect a new religious house, he may not proced in the matter without first obtaining the permission of the local Ordinary in whose territory the house is to be established. For the establishment of an exempt religious house, whether formal or not, and of all religious houses in territories still under the jurisdiction of the Sacred Propaganda, the approval of the Holy See, as well as the consent of the Ordinary of the place, are required.[15]

This authorization granted by the local Ordinary or by the Sacred Propaganda is given in the form of a written document, although such documents are not required for the validity of the erection of the house, (canon 11).[16]

After the local Ordinary has granted his approbation, the competent religious superior may then proceed to the actual erection of the religious house. Canonists disagree as to whether or not a formal decree of canonical erection must necessarily be issued by the religious superior in order to erect juridically a religious house. Some

---

[14] *Normae* of 1901, arts. 271, 272, 305.

[15] Can. 497, § 1.

[16] Larraona, "Commentarium Codicis"—*CpR*, XII (1931), 249.

maintain that the mere fact of establishing the house, or of recognizing it as part of the institute, is sufficient for canonical erection.[17] Coronata, on the other hand, believes that a formal decree of erection is necessary.[18]

Brisebois claims that when the competent religious superior and the proper ecclesiastical authority mutually cooperate to fulfill the conditions of the law, all that is necessary is a manifestation, in some manner, of the will of the superior.[19] The Code does not mention the necessity of a formal decree for the erection of a religious house. The only requirements necessary on the part of the religious superior to erect a religious house are a clear and certain manifestation of his intention to erect such a house and the actual erection of the house. Therefore, the simple fact that a religious superior assigns a certain number of members to a house is sufficient action on his part to consider the house formally established and endowed with moral personality.[20]

The canonical argument for this opinion is based on canon 100, § 1. This canon states that moral personality is granted in one of two ways; either by a formal decree issued by the competent superior or by prescription of the law. However, religious superiors of non-exempt institutes are unable to grant a formal decree since they have no jurisdiction in the external forum and therefore their decree

---

17 "Nec sit necessarium *decretum formale* erectionis, quod nullibi Praescriptum invenitur (tale certe non ut praevius consensus Ordinarii aut S. Sedis), nec etsi datum esset, sufficeret ad personalitatem concedendam quando agitur de Religionibus non exemptis. Facta erectione, id est statuta communitate et agnita ut domus Religionis, ipsi personalitas, ac proinde capacitas, *ex jure* obvenit."—Larraona, "Commentarium Codicis"—*CpR,* XII (1931), 249.

18 Decretum igitur erectionis, quod necessarium putamus, non ab Ordinario nec a S. Sede, sed generatim ab ipsa religione dandum erit vel a provincia juxta constitutiones."—Coronata, *Institutiones,* I, p. 620, n. 522.

19 Brisebois, *De Natura Juridica Domus Religiosae,* p. 45; Bouscaren, *Canon Law Digest,* I, 152.

20 "Ad domum vero constitutendam sufficit voluntas auctoritatis competentis externo actu manifestata, cum debitis licentiis: quibus positis, 'ex ipso juris praescripto', domus qualitatem personae moralis consequitur."—Vromant, *De Bonis Ecclesiae Temporalibus,* p. 208.

can hardly confer the moral personality upon the house. On the other hand, the approval of the Holy See and the consent of the Ordinary required by canon 497, § 1, do not seem to contain such a formal decree granting moral personality. Therefore, since no true religious house may exist without being a moral person, it logically follows that the moral personality is granted by the prescription of the law itself.[21]

### ARTICLE 2. THE RIGHT OF OWNERSHIP OF A RELIGIOUS HOUSE

Canon 531 asserts the right of all religious houses to acquire and own temporal goods, unless their capacity be excluded or restricted by the rules and constitutions. From the moment of its erection every religious house, whether it be of pontifical or diocesan right, enjoys the capacity to acquire and to possess temporal goods.[22] This right of ownership may be restricted or modified by the particular law of the institute. Larraona states that almost all possible varieties of restrictions are found among the religious institutes of the Church.[23] Thus, the Friars Minors and the Capuchins have not been permitted to own property since the time of the council of Trent. According to the constitutions of the Discalced Carmelites, houses not destined for missions are allowed to have their own income only in certain cases.[24]

Actually, at least five systems of ownership of temporal goods by religious institutes can be discerned.[25] First, there is the system of total independence which is the monastic type of ownership. This

---

21 Brisebois, *De Natura Juridica Domus Religiosae,* p. 45: "Facta erectione, id est statuta communitate et agnita ut domus Religionis, ipsi personalitas, ac proinde capacitas, *ex jure* obvenit."—Larraona, "Commentarium Codicis"—*CpR,* XII (1931), 249.

22 Can. 1495.

23 Larraona, "Commentarium Codicis"—*CpR,* XII (1931), 251.

24 Larraona, "Commentarium Codicis"—*CpR,* XII (1931) 251.

25 Gutierrez, "Quaestiones Canonicae Circa Bona Ecclesiastica"—*Acta et Documenta Congressus Generalis de Statibus Perfectionis* (4 vols., Romae: Editiones Paulinae, 1950), I, 557 (hereinafter cited as *Acta et Documenta*).

system, similar to the allodial type of civil law,[26] is practiced in monasteries *sui juris* of the same monastic order, and consists in the total independence of each monastery.

A second system is that of contributions. This system of ownership is used in several religious orders. It is substantially the same as the monastic system with the following variations: a contribution is periodically exacted from each individual house for the purpose of supporting the provincial and general curias. It does not admit the transfer of goods from one house to another without the permission of the local superior. Generally, the goods belong to the individual houses themselves. The province and the order possess a so-called *depositum provinciae vel ordinis* composed of money, deeds, and titles *constituted by money* contributed by the local houses to defray the expenses of the province, or money contributed by the local houses and provinces to defray the expenses of the order. The provincial bursar is not entitled by law to represent the individual houses of the province without the consent or mandate of the proper local superior, or, at least, without consulting the local superior; nor can the general bursar do so without a similar mandate, or consultation. The Dominicans and the Jesuits seem to adhere to a form of this system.

A third system is that of a coordinated autonomy. Each moral person acquires and possesses its goods independently. The annual surplus of each house, however, is annually taxed by the province, and the surplus of the provinces is taxed by the institute.[27] Most religious congregations adhere to this system mentioned in the *Normae* of 1901.[28]

---

[26] This is a system whereby land is held in absolute independence without being subject to any rent, service or acknowledgment to a superior. It is opposed to the feudal system.

[27] *The Constitutions and Rules of the Congregation of the Missionary Oblates of the Most Holy and Immaculate Virgin Mary* (Rome: 1945), arts. 435, 20°, 531, 12°.

[28] "Quaelibet domus, copia rerum abundans, quotannis ex eo quod in fine anni, rationibus consolidatis, et omnibus deductis expensis, superest pecuniae, tertiam partem tradat capsae provinciali, et quaelibet provincia eodem modo tertiam partem eorum quae sibi supersunt, tradat arcae Instituti".—*Normae* of 1901, art. 294.

A fourth system might be called that of subordinated autonomy. According to this form of administration, each inferior moral person owns and administers temporalities in its own name. The rights of ownership and of administration, however, are subordinated to the common good of all the houses of the institute. The amount of mutual assistance is not rigidly determined. In this system, the moral persons themselves possess and are responsible for the administration of their temporal goods, but the capacity to acquire, or better, the right to retain and to use property is limited and subordinated to the common good of all the houses. A certain administrative centralization is adhered to according to the diverse congregations which practice this system.

The fifth and last system is that of centralized property. The congregation only has the right to possess, and it is responsible for the subordinate moral persons in the congregation. To this system of property, one may assimilate the system whereby the right of ownership is centralized on a lower level, in a province, rather than in the institute as a whole. In this instance, the property belongs to the province and not to the congregation.[29]

The juridical capacity of local houses to acquire and to possess may be modified or totally prohibited by the constitutions of the individual congregations.[30] Here, as always, must be applied the rule of law: *generi per speciem derogatur.*[31] The limitation may be either total, when the rules deny the right of property to the individual house; or it may be partial, when the constitutions limit the right of property and that of acquisition. This restriction may concern either the goods themselves, or the validity and liceity of certain acts.[32]. It must be noted, however, that each local religious house is presumed to enjoy the right of ownership, and that the restriction or limitation of this right must be proven and must accrue from a legitimate source. If the constitutions are silent on this matter, and do

---

29 For a more detailed explanation of these five systems of ownership, cf. Gutierrez, "Quaestiones Canonicae Circa Bona Ecclesiastica"—*Acta et Documenta,* I, 557.

30 Can. 531.

31 Reg. 34, R.J. in VI°.

32 Larraona, "Commentarium Codicis"—*CpR,* XII (1931), 251.

not limit in any way the right of property, each house enjoys the full extent of ownership mentioned in canon 531. This right is exercised, however, in accordance with the particular custom or practice of the community in regard to the administration of temporal goods.[33]

Although local houses enjoy the right of property as stated above, the exercise of this right is subject to certain restrictions. The Pre-Code law stated that: each house must give one third of its surplus funds to the province at the end of the fiscal year; each province, in turn, must give one third of its annual surplus to the general fund of the institute.[34] It is the actual practice of the Sacred Congregation of Religious to permit each institute to determine the amount of the annual surplus that each house must turn over to the province.[35] To determine the net surplus, allowance is to be made for interest to be paid on the capital of a debt, as well as for the sum necessary to amortize existing debts that the house may have to bear. More will be said of this problem in the chapter concerning major religious superiors.[36] If particular law and custom are silent regarding the disposition of surplus funds, it seems unlawful to prohibit a local superior from creating a reserve fund for the local house or to demand that he give the entire surplus of the fiscal year to the province or to the institute. To impose such an obligation would offend against; 1) the relative independence that the common law grants each house; 2) the security of a local house by demanding that it partake of the financial risks of the mother-house; 3) and possibly against the intention of particular benefactors who might wish to favor the good works of a certain house.[37]

It is expected that local houses will cooperate with the province for the common good of the province, and that the province, in turn

---

[33] Schaefer, *De Religiosis,* p. 410, n. 187.

[34] *Nomae* of 1901, art. 294.

[35] Gutierrez, *art. cit.—Acta et Documenta,* I, 559.

[36] Cf. chapter V, art. 3 p. 96.

[37] Creusen, *Religieux et Religieuses* (Paris: Desclée, 1950), n. 159; Battandier, *Guide Canonique,* n. 474.

will contribute to the works of the entire congregation. This is especially true in the case of institutes which must give a long and intensive course of training to their subjects and of those institutes which accept undertakings in the mission fields.

In recent years, the Holy See has approved constitutions which impose upon local houses or provinces contributions greater than those exacted by the *Normae* of 1901. At times, the annual amount of contributions is left to the judgment of the general chapter or to the superior general with the approbation of his council.[38]

---

[38] Creusen, *op. cit.*, n. 159.

# CHAPTER III

## The Authority of the Local Religious Superior in Temporal Matters

### Article 1. The Source of His Authority

Since the right of ownership of a religious house resides in the moral person itself, and since moral persons are physically incapable of administering temporal property, it is necessary that the administration of religious houses be entrusted to physical persons, i. e. administrators. Obviously, the administration of the goods of a local religious house cannot be entrusted to each individual religious since such a procedure would be contrary to the good order so necessary in such a matter. Moreover, since the community itself cannot immediately exercise this administration, it is necessary that administrators be named to supervise the distribution and the use of temporal goods owned by the moral person.[1]

Naturally, no individual religious may usurp the right of administration. Since each community has the right to own and to administer its own goods—unless particular law has made some restrictions in this matter—the administrators receive their right of administration from the owner of the goods they administer. That owner is none other than the community itself whose will is manifested in the constitutions.[2]

The immediate administration of a religious house belongs to the local superior. This right stems from his dominative power mentioned in canon 501, § 1 of the Code of Canon Law. In every society, some kind of authority must exist whereby the members are directed to the attainment of the end of the society. Such authority necessarily inheres in the very nature of a society and resides in the lawful

---

[1] Suarez, *De Religione,* Tract. VIII, lib. II, c. 26, n. 1—*Opera Omnia,* XVI, 241. Although some moral persons can sometimes act by themselves, i.e. *collegialiter,* they still require special administrators for the management of their temporal goods.

[2] Suarez, *De Religione,* Tract. VIII, lib. II, c. 26, n. 2—*Opera Omnia,* XVI, 242.

head of that society who has been selected to direct its members. Consequently, the nature of a society gives rise to the authority in its superiors, and also determines the nature of the authority itself. Superiors and chapters of exempt clerical institutes enjoy a power of jurisdiction conceded by the Church through canonical mission. Superiors of non-exempt clerical institutes, on the other hand, enjoy a dominative power "whereby they can govern and direct the actions of their subjects to the attainment of the end of the community".[3] The local superior of a non-exempt religious house enjoys such a dominative power since he is the head of an imperfect society lawfully established by the Church.

Some authors have maintained that the basis of this power lies in the vow of obedience which the religious profess on entering the religious state.[4] However, if such were the case, the subjects would confer the authority upon their religious superior and could grant to the superior the right to give commands that would be publicly recognized by the Church. Since such a theory does not seem acceptable, it is preferable to maintain that the dominative power of superiors has its foundation in the fact that the non-exempt congregation is a society lawfully recognized by the Church as an imperfect society.[5]

The very nature of the dominative power enjoyed by the local superior of a non-exempt institute requires not only that he regulate the personal actions of the individual members, but also that he concern himself with the management of the temporal goods that are owned in common by the religious house. This opinion is held by McGrath,[6] although Kindt maintains that the administration of temporal goods by the local superior involves the use of a power different from dominative power because canon 501, § 1 refers only

---

[3] McGrath, *The Local Superior in Non-Exempt Clerical Congregations*, p. 47.

[4] Coronata, *Institutiones*, I, p. 634, n. 534.

[5] For an extensive study of this subject, cf. McGrath, *The Local Superior in Non-Exempt Clerical Congregations*, pp. 39-59.

[6] McGrath, *op. cit.*, p. 57.

to the subjects of the superior and not to the temporal goods of the moral person.[7] Such acts of administration certainly have reference to the subjects of the superior since the superior is dealing with the temporal goods possessed by them as a moral unit.

## ARTICLE 2. THE DISTINCTION BETWEEN ORDINARY AND EXTRAORDINARY ADMINISTRATION OF TEMPORAL GOODS

The acts of administration performed by the local superior and other officials are many and diverse. These acts may be divided into different classes, based on various criteria. The most important distinction, however, is the one between the acts of *ordinary* administration and acts of *extraordinary* administration. This distinction derives its importance from the fact that particular officials and superiors act validly or invalidly depending on the ordinary or extraordinary nature of the administrative act. The Code, in at least two canons, alludes to this division of acts of administration. Canon 532, § 2 states that superiors and other officials may validly perform acts of ordinary administration within the limits of their office. Canon 1527, § 1 states that administrators act invalidly if they go beyond the end and mode of ordinary administration unless they have previously obtained the permission of the Ordinary of the place. This canon has reference, therefore, to a class of extraordinary administrative acts.

The Code merely states the distinction between these two classes of acts performed in the administration of temporal goods, but does not define either category; nor does it give a criterion to distinguish the one type from the other. In their attempts to differentiate such types of administrative acts, authors have had recourse to various criteria which are not always adequate. It is of the utmost importance and necessity, therefore, to establish the standard by which acts of ordinary administration may be distinguished from acts of extraordinary administration, so that superiors may know whether they

---

[7] Kindt, *De Potestate Dominative in Religione,* Universitas Catholica Lovaniensis Dissertationes, Series II, Tomus 34 (Brugis Parisiis-Romae: Desclée de Brower, 1945), p. 342.

act validly or invalidly in particular instances. The constitutions of each religious community usually provide particular norms to direct superiors in such matters, and they frequently contain an enumeration of acts belonging to each class. In some instances, however, doubts may arise by reason of circumstances not foreseen by the constitutions. If he is to solve his doubt in such cases, the superior must have recourse to an ultimate basis of distinction between these two classes of administrative acts.

Canonists have proposed many criteria to distinguish these two classes of administrative acts, such as the frequent, either daily or periodic, recurrence of the acts; the necessity of the permission of a major superior; the nature of the office of the superior of the religious house; and finally, the object and the mode of administration. In the view of the present writer, the last mentioned theory seems to have the most merit and appears more acceptable than the three preceding ones.

To distinguish between ordinary and extraordinary administration, many authors propose as a criterion the frequency of the administrative acts; that is, the daily or periodic recurrence of such acts.[8] They maintain that those acts performed daily or periodically pertain to ordinary administration, while administrative acts that do not occur daily or at regular intervals belong to extraordinary administration. But this standard may not be valid in every case, since certain acts of ordinary administration are not necessarily performed daily, nor even at short term intervals. Though most acts of ordinary administration do occur frequently, and acts of extraordinary administration infrequently, yet, there may be acts of ordinary administration which occur infrequently; for example, the repair of an automobile.

---

[8] Coronata, *Instiutiones,* I, p. 678, n. 559; Regatillo, *Institutiones Juris Canonici* (2 vols., Santander: "Sal Terrae", 1951), II, 173 (hereinafter cited as *Institutiones*); Vermeersch-Creusen, *Epitome Juris Canonici cum Commentariis ad Scholas et ad Usum Privatum* (3 vols., Vol. I, 3 ed., 1927; Vol. II, 2 ed., 1925; Vol. III, 2 ed., 1925, Mechlinae-Romae: Dessain), II, n. 655.

A second group of authors proposes that the distinction between ordinary and extraordinary administration be based on the necessity to seek a permission from a major superior before performing the act. According to this opinion, those acts of administration are of an ordinary nature which may be performed without any special permission; those acts which may be performed only with permission of a higher superior are of an extraordinary nature.[9]

If this criterion is examined closely, it is found to contain serious flaws. If these authors maintain that acts of extraordinary administration are those whose *liceity* depends on the permission of a higher superior, their position is certainly untenable. Certain acts, performed without this previous permission are valid, and are recognized as acts of ordinary administration by the Code. Canon 532, § 2 states that superiors and officials of a local house designated by the constitutions can, within the limits of their office, perform validly the juridical acts of ordinary administration. Canon 1527, § 1 states the same principle negatively, saying that officials who exceed the limits of ordinary administration without the permission of the Ordinary act invalidly.[10] One may conclude therefore that administrative acts performed validly by the local superior or other officials are of ordinary administration. Therefore, even though permission is required for the liceity of certain acts of administration, and though they be executed without this formality, they remain valid. It is evident that either the constitutions or the religious superiors can require local superiors and officials to obtain a special permission before performing certain administrative acts; such instances are

---

[9] Wernz-Vidal say that acts of ordinary administration are those *qui ab administratoribus poni possunt sine praescripto praevio recursu ad altiorem auctoritatem.*—Wernz—Vidal, *Jus Canonicum ad Codicis Norman Exactum,* 7 tomes in 8 (Romae: Apud Aedes Universitatis Gregorianae, 1923-1938), II, 212: Augustine mentions that "acts of ordinary administration are such as occur frequently and are performed without special formalities".—Augustine, *A Commentary of the New Code of Canon Law* (8 vols., Vols. VI-VIII, 2 ed., 1922-1924; Vols. III-V, 3 ed., 1922-1923; Vols. I-II, 4 ed., 1921-1923, St. Louis, Herder), III, 179.

[10] For the application of canons 1518-1551 to the administration of religious property, cf. pp. 94-97.

frequent in religious life. However, these acts remain in the realm of ordinary administration whenever permission is required for liceity only.

If these authors propose as a criterion that an act is of an extraordinary nature because its *validity* depends on the permission of a higher superior, their opinion still does not seem to provide the ultimate norm of distinction. Canon 532, § 2 might seem to confirm the opinion of this class of authors. They reason thus: the canon states that acts of ordinary administration may be performed validly by legitimate superiors and officials provided they act within the scope of their powers.[11] If permission of a higher superior is necessary for the validity of a specific act, one may conclude that such an act is one of an extraordinary nature. And if one combines a number of such cases where permission of the major superiors is required for the validity of an act, he may, by a process of induction, form an approximate notion of extraordinary administration as understood by the Church.

Moreover, this particular criterion which bases the distinction between acts of ordinary and extraordinary administration in the necessity of consultations with major superiors seems to lead one into a vicious circle. If such an opinion were maintained, canons 532, § 2 and 1527 § 1 would be tautological. If acts of ordinary administration are defined as those acts validly performed by authorized persons without a permission of a higher superior, canon 532, § 2 would be solemnly affirming that superiors and officials may accomplish validly without permission of major superiors all administrative acts which do not require a permission for their validity.

Therefore, it is evident that this criterion may only serve as a sign *a posteriori*. The necessity of a permission from a higher superior for the validity of an administrative act is a *consequence rather than a cause of the extraordinary nature of the act.* Thus, if a permission

---

11 This canon says nothing about the permission from a *major* superior, nor does it make a distinction between the superiors. The determination is left entirely to the constitutions of the community. Presumably an econome could perform some acts validly only with the permission of the local superior if the constitutions set up this arrangement.

from a higher superior is required for the validity of an act, one may conclude that the act is of an extraordinary nature; but it may not be maintained that an act is of an extraordinary nature because a permission is required for its validity.

A third opinion is that of Huot.[12] He proposes, as the ultimate criterion, the nature of the office of an administrator. According to his definition, ordinary administration is that which is contained within the limits of the office of the administrator, whereas extraordinary administration is that administration which exceeds the limits of the office.[13] He supports his opinion by citing canon 532, § 2 where it is said that superiors and officials act validly within the limits of their office: *intra fines sui muneris.* He then explains that the office of an administrator in a religious institute consists in the conservation and amelioration of the stable capital of that institute. Whenever the exercise of the power of *dominium* over capital assets is necessary, the ordinary administrator may not act without a special permission. He then says that acts which surpass the limits of the office of the religious administrator are those that modify or change the actual state of stable capital.[14] Huot's opinion seems not in accord with the law of the Code for the following reasons:

a) The author appears to maintain that administration is concerned only with stable capital, for he makes no mention of free capital or its administration;

b) Not every administrative act that concerns the conservation, amelioration and productivity of stable capital is necessarily an act of ordinary administration. According to this opinion, the repairs of a deteriorated roof or of a damaged building would be acts of ordinary administration, although the cost of such repairs might easily surpass the scope of authority of a local superior. Superiors and officials would therefore perform validly such acts without previous

---

[12] Huot, *art. cit.—CpRM,* XXXIV (1955), 61-62.

[13] "Administration ordinaria est illa quae continetur in potestate seu intra limites muneris administratoris; extraordinaria vero, quae hos limites transgreditur." Huot, *art. cit.—CpRM,* XXXIV (1955), 61.

[14] Administratio extraordinairia est illa quae ordinatur ad modificationem ipsius patrimonii stabilis." Huot, *art. cit.—CpRM,* XXXIV (1955), 61.

permission of major superiors, since canon 532, § 2 validates every act of ordinary administration.

c) It seems untenable to limit the definition of extraordinary administration to those acts alone which modify the *actual state of the stable capital* of the institute. Huot's definition implies that every administrative act concerning *free capital* is validly performed by superiors and officials no matter what the amount involved may be. The constitutions of most religious institutes, however, limit the powers of local superiors and their officials with respect to their rights over free capital. They stipulate that the superiors and officials may not spend validly more than a certain amount without the consent of a higher superior who may at times be even obliged to consult his council for advice and consent.

d) The author also implies the possibility that certain acts of ordinary administration may not be performed validly without a previous permission.[15] But, if a permission is required for the validity of an administrative act, the act is *ipso facto* of an extraordinary nature, since canon 532, § 2 validates every act of ordinary administration that is performed by superiors and other officials.

A fourth category of authors give no criterior whatsoever to distinguish one type of administration from the other, but proceed by enumerating the acts proper to each class.[16] Obviously, this procedure may be useful, but it does not answer the question regarding the specific nature of the ultimate criterion.

The above-mentioned criteria seem neither adequate nor in perfect conformity with the Code, although all of them have some degree of merit, in so far as they offer some basis of distinction.

A last criterion to distinguish acts of ordinary and extraordinary administration, and one which seems to this writer to be the most plausible, calls upon the notion of the OBJECT and MODE of administration (*finis et modus*), the object being the end and purpose of a given act, and the mode being the measure and method to

---

15 "Administratio ordinaria . . . si licentia requiritur, *normaliter* non erit ad valorem." Huot, *art. cit.—CpRM*, XXXIV (1955), 61.

16 Naz, *Traité de Droit Canonique* (4 vols., 2 ed., Paris: Letouzey et Ané, 1955), III, 245.

be followed by the religious superior and officials in performing it. The ultimate criterion used to distinguish both classes of administrative acts and to determine the limits and the rights of administrators is found in the OBJECT and in the MODE of the management of the goods involved. Canon 1527, § 1 mentions that acts of extraordinary administration are those which go beyond the object and mode of ordinary administration.

The OBJECT of administration of temporal goods in religious houses is the maintenance, productivity and amelioration of property. This object includes within its scope the contracting of expenses necessary for the upkeep of the religious subjects according to their way of religious life.[17] The MODE in which the temporal administration is conducted refers to the manner in which the acts are performed; for example, buying wholesale or retail, buying a daily supply or a yearly supply.

Ordinary administration, then, comprises the aggregate of administrative acts required for the current maintenance of property and personnel of the religious house, and therefore constitutes a preestablished and permanent order of economic activities approved by competent authorities. The administrator, be he superior or official, is thus empowered to provide for the support of persons and the maintenance of property of the moral person. The provision of food, of clothing, of repairs and renewal of household goods come under his ordinary powers. These are administrative acts currently needed for the habitual upkeep of the religious house and are marked by a moral continuity and by a certain frequency which may vary according to the nature of the things to be bought.

Consequently, a stable order of economic activities is constituted, a preestablished order which has the general approval of the competent authority upon whom devolves the right of supervising and of modifying this order, if circumstances so warrant. That is why superiors and officials of religious houses, in virtue of this general

[17] Ordinaria administratio comprehendit actus illos qui regulariter necessarii aestimantur ad res, fructus, bona conservanda et normalibus necessitatibus subveniendum."—Larraona, "Commentarium Codicis"—*CpR,* XII (1931), 356.

approbation, may exercise their duties without special permission for each particular case. This general approbation may be given either explicitly or implicitly; explicitly, if the major superior defines precisely the scope of the administrative powers of local superiors and of treasurers; implicitly, if the major superior, being fully cognizant of certain administrative acts, approves them or even tolerates them indirectly by approving the accounts rendered by the administrators of the local house. This stable order of economic activities is required by common law which states at least the general principles, (Can. 532 § 2) but it is determined more completely and adequately by the constitutions. This order is also established in part by custom, and lastly by major superiors who may be called upon to give additional precision, especially concerning the mode of administration.

Extraordinary administration, on the other hand, consists of those acts that are not currently necessary for the day to day maintenance of personnel and temporal assets of the religious house, and therefore are not comprised in the order of economic activities preestablished and duly sanctioned by the competent authorities.[18] These acts go beyond the object of ordinary administration of temporal goods and are not therefore included in the ordinary powers of the local superiors and other officials.

In fact, however, certain difficulties may arise in determining whether or not a specific act is currently necessary for the well-being of the religious moral person, and, therefore, one of ordinary administration. In such cases, one must consider not only the object of the act (whether it is necessary for the habitual upkeep of persons and things), but also its mode or its circumstances. It is possible that a specific act pertain to extraordinary administration by reason of its mode, but not by reason of its object. An example of such an act is the purchase of food. In view of its object, this administrative act belongs to the category of ordinary administration since it is necessary for the current upkeep of the religious house. But if the act involves, for instance, the purchase of a quantity sufficient for two or three months, this procedure may not be the normal mode approved

---

18 Gutierrez, "Notio actus ordinarii et actus extraordinarii administrationis" —*Acta et Documenta,* I, 564.

by higher superiors, or by the constitutions. In this event the act may possibly need to be considered in the realm of extraordinary administration.

In order that an act be classified as one of ordinary administration, it must be such both in view of its OBJECT and its MODE. Otherwise, it must be classified as an act of extraordinary administration.[19] It is evident that acts of ordinary or extraordinary administration distinguished on the basis of OBJECT and MODE may differ with each institute, since the constitutions and practices of each religious community are the ultimate determining factor in this matter.[20] Some constitutions may empower local superiors to spend as much as three hundred dollars without permission of the council or of higher superiors; whereas, the constitutions of other institutes may permit local superiors to spend a maximum of only seventy-five dollars without permission. Therefore, the objects of ordinary administration in different communities may be diverse.[21] This same norm also applies to the mode of administrative acts. Since the Code only mentions that superiors and officials may perform acts of ordinary administration without placing any limit to their powers, it remains for the constitutions to determine more precisely the object and extent of each class of administrative acts. Particular law may determine that certain acts, regardless of their nature, belong to extraordinary administration.[22]

---

[19] Larraona, "Commentarium Codicis"—*CpR,* XII (1931), 357, note 484.

[20] "Actus *extraordinarii* non abstracte sed concrete, pro singularum administrationum fine et modo sunt determinandi; munus administratoris ejusque facultates non abstracte sed ex Constitutionibus desumenda sunt; idem actus pro hac administratione vel in hac Religione potest esse ordinarius, in aliis potest esse extraordinarius".—Gutierrez, *art. cit.—Acta et Documenta,* I, 564.

[21] "Actus ordinarii aliqui habentur quidem in jure canonico descripti; sed praecipue definiendi sunt ex jure particulari. Hoc jus particulare munus singulorum administratorum potest libere circumscribere et eorum facultates libere delimitare, juxta fines administrationis et modum in ea gerenda observandum"—Gutierrez, *art. cit.—Acta et Documenta,* I, 564-565.

[22] " . . . quia agitur de conceptu juridico, legislatio, sive generalis, sive particularis, in concreto non raro determinant expresse quinam hi actus sint et fines ac modum intra quosquos tales reputantur."—Larraona, "Commentarium Codicis"—*CpR,* XII (1931), 356.

Despite the norms established by the constitutions, custom, etc., some unforeseen cases may arise for which there is no precedent. In such cases, it pertains to the various qualified authorities to decide which acts are to be considered as extraordinary.[23] This intervention of authority is especially desirable in questions concerning the *mode* of administrative acts. Changed circumstances may make it desirable to consider as ordinary an expense which was considered extraordinary in the past; v.g., buying wholesale quantities of food that can be preserved by modern refrigeration methods. Apart from exceptional cases, however, superiors may not arbitrarily determine the ordinary or extraordinary nature of an act.

Right reason demands that particular law should not be too rigid in fixing the limits of ordinary administration, but should grant freedom to superiors sufficient to avoid too frequent recourse to higher authorities for permission. If particular law is too restrictive in this domain, the entire management of local houses may be unreasonably impeded and even rendered ineffective. On the other hand, particular law ought not to be too lenient since some control must be kept over all acts of administration.[24]

This last opinion, which is upheld by Gutierrez and Larraona[25] seems more plausible than the preceding ones. It takes into account certain elements of the preceding criteria but without their objectionable features. It is better, then, in the view of the present writer, to maintain that ordinary administration be determined by a pre-established and permanent order approved by competent authorities for each particular religious house, and that extraordinary administration include the administrative acts that go either beyond the object of ordinary administration or beyond the mode determined by the competent authorities. By virtue of their mandate, the local superior and other officials proceed validly without explicit authorization in respect to acts of ordinary administration. Concerning

---

[23] Larraona, "Commentarium Codicis"—*CpR,* XII, (1931), 357, note 484.

[24] *Sanctae Romanae Rotae Decisiones seu Sententiae,* XXXI (1939), 355-359.

[25] Gutierrez, *art. cit.*—*Acta et Documenta,* I, 563-565; Larranona, "Commentarium Codicis"—*CpR,* XII (1931), 356.

extraordinary administration, however, the local superior and other officials may not act validly without the previous consent of the legitimate superior.

### ARTICLE 3. THE LOCAL SUPERIOR AND ORDINARY ADMINISTRATION

Before determining the powers of the local superior in the ordinary administration of a local religious house, some mention must be made of the applicability of canons 1518-1551 to the administration of religious goods. The immediate legislation concerning the administration of religious property is found in canons 531-537. The norms contained therein have binding force on all religious administrators and anything contrary to the norms contained in these canons has no binding force whatsoever on religious administrators. The next source of such legislation is found in the particular constitutions of each individual religious community. Canon 532 § 1 specifically states that the property of the institute, of the province and of the houses is to be administered in conformity with the constitutions of the individual religious communities, thereby canonizing the legislation of the constitutions and rendering such legislation obligatory for all religious. Consequently, the prescriptions contained in the sixth section of the third book of the Code that are contrary to the norms found in the two preceding sources have no binding force whatsoever on religious administrators. The rule of law *generi per speciem derogatur*[26] is operative in such cases.

As a general rule, however, the canons regulating the administration of religious property must not be considered in isolation from the canons concerning the administration of ecclesiastical goods in general. The majority of authors are of the opinion that canons 1518-1551 do apply in some ways to the administration of religious property.[27]

---

[26] Reg. 34, R.J. in VI°

[27] "Lex communis de bonis ecclesiasticis continetur can. 1495-1543, in jure religiosorum vero praeterea observandi sunt can. 531-537".—Pejska, *Jus Canonicum Religiosorum* (3 ed., Brigurgi-Brisgoviae: 1927), p. 58; "Praescripta praesentis canonis 1523 sunt generatim dicta de administratoribus bonorum ecclesasticorum; sed in quantum religiosis applicari possunt, etiam pro eis certo valent, cum et bona religionis sint bona ecclesiastica."—Fanfani, *De*

The binding force of legislation, applicable to the administration of religious houses, contained in canons 1518-1528 and not contrary to canons 531-537 must be established by the following rules:

1) The canons that explicitly mention the religious or are included in the legislation concerning the administration of religious property have force of law for all religious administrators.[28]

2) According to canon 20, canons other than those discussed above will be applicable to religious only by analogy of law in instances where the legislation proper to the religious contains no law governing the matter in question.[29] In such cases the rights and duties attributed to the local Ordinary must be transferred to a major religious superior.[30]

3) Finally, since canon 618, § 2 exempts strictly religious property of pontifical institutes from the jurisdiction of the local Ordinary, canons mentioning the ecclesiastical administrators and requiring the permission of the local Ordinary to posit certain acts concerning

---

*Jure Religiosorum ad normam Codicis Juris Canonici* (3 ed., Rovigo: 1949), p. 226, n. 154; "Singuli autem bonorum . . . domus religiosae administratores, proprie et formaliter sunt administratores bonorum ecclesiasticorum (cfr. can. 1497, § 1) ; et idcirco in munere suo implendo praescripta servare tenentur quae in cann. 1522-1528 generaliter statuuntur de omnibus administratoribus bonorum ecclesiasticorum, quamvis propriis eorum cujusque Superioribus jura tribuenda sint quae ibidem Ordinario loci tribuuntur."—Berutti, *Institutiones Juris Canonici* (6 vols., Taurni-Romae: 1936), III, 115; "In libro III Codicis I. C. ad titulum 28, partis VI, canones 1518-1528 de *omnibus bonis ecclesiasticis in genere decernunt,* etiam quae habentur in potestate religiosorum. Uti tamen conjicitur e contextu, a variis praescriptis excipiuntur bona quae ad religiones, praesertim juris pontificii pertinent."—Vromant, *De Bonis Ecclesiae Temporalibus,* p. 165, n. 187.

28 Cf. cans. 1524, 530; "Adsunt alique in citato titulo quae Religiosos ex ipsi textu Codicis tangunt."—Larraona, "Commentarium Codicis.—*CpR,* XII (1931), 355.

29 " . . . alia quae ex juridica *saltem* analogia ceterisque regulis can.-20 applicanda sunt (cfr. CC. 1518, § 1 col. ad can. 518, § 2; 1523, 1528),"—Larraona, "Commentarium Codicis"—*CpR,* XII (1931), 355.

30 " . . . quamvis proprius eorum cujusque Superioribus jura tribuenda sint quae ibidem Ordinario loci tribuuntur."—Berutti, *Institutiones Juris Canonici,* III, 115.

the administration of such property have no binding force for religious of pontifical institutes.[31]

Furthermore, the letters and declarations of the Sacred Congregation of the Council concerning the administration of ecclesiastical goods have no binding force for religious administrators, although they contain very prudent norms that must be considered as very useful for religious.[32]

Once the distinction has been drawn between acts of ordinary and of extraordinary administration in a religious house, and the relation between canons 1518-1551 and canons 531-537 established, the rights and duties of the local superior concerning each class of administrative acts may be more easily determined.

According to canon 532, § 2, the local superior has the right to contract expenses and to perform juridical acts of ordinary administration. These acts will usually concern the upkeep of the personnel and of the property of the local religious house. In general, he should administer the goods of the religious house just as a prudent *paterfamilias* administers the goods of his family. He must exercise the diligence and close attention to husbanding the patrimony entrusted to his care that a father would show caring for the economic well-being of his family.[33]

By virtue of his ordinary powers, the local superior may acquire property by investment and receive the rents due to the religious house from those using the property which belongs to it. The superior has the right to accept gifts if they are for the furtherance of

---

[31] "In religionibus tamen juris pontificii Ordinario loci non licet: 1° . . . de re oeconomica cognoscere, salvo praescripto can. 533-535."—can. 618 §2.

[32] "Sed licet ejusmodi dispositiones, declarationes, litterae . . . S. C. Concilii circa bona ecclesiastica non teneant religiosos - et haec est norma certa tenenda - tamen continent optima criteria religiosis etiam valde utilia. Ita, ex. gr. interpretatio can. 1532, quam S.C. Concilii saepe inculcavit comprehendens inter actus alienationis . . a religiosis prae oculis habenda est." Gutierrez, "Adnotationes"—*CpR,* XXXII (1953), 162.

[33] Cf. can. 1523. "Canon 1523 non immediate Religiosos tangit, potius ex juridica analogia eis applicandus est."—Schaefer, *De Religiosis,* p. 417, n. 194

divine cult or for any other religious or charitable purpose, provided that these gifts do not burden the local house with obligations.[34]

The local superior has the positive obligation imposed by the virtue of justice to take all measures necessary for the conservation of the property entrusted to his care. He may therefore take out insurance and pay just and sufficient wages to the hired help. If the conservation entails extraordinary expenses, the superior must first obtain the necessary permission required for the validity of the act. Not only must he diligently conserve the goods themselves, but he must also keep in good order and in good condition the documents on which the rights of the religious house are based.[35] Canon 1523 serves as an excellent norm to be followed by all religious administrators and the jurisprudence of the Sacred Congregation of Religious has made these norms practically obligatory.[36]

In addition to the local superior, every single religious assigned to a religious house has a certain duty concerning the property of that house. On the one hand, a religious may not misuse, damage or squander the property of the community. This obligation arises from the vow of poverty and also from the virtue of justice, since these goods do not belong to him personally. On the other hand, he may be bound in charity to take action concerning the conservation of such property. However, this duty is ordinarily discharged by calling pertinent matters to the attention of the superior or treasurer.[37]

Vromant gives an excellent summary of the acts of administration which a local superior may perform without permission of a higher superior:[38]

a) the collection and banking of money acquired in approved ways;

b) the collection of debts from creditors;

c) the collection of annual income from stocks, shares, or bonds;

---

34 If the donor requires some compensation for the gift, the local superior may have to consult the legitimate authorities and obtain their consent.

35 Cf. can. 1523, 6°.

36 Huot, *art. cit.*—*CpRM*, XXXIII (1954), 326-327; "Elenchus quaestionum pro relatione quinquennali", art. 87—Bouscaren, *Canon Law Digest*, III, 174.

37 Suarez, *De Religione*, Tract. VIII, lib. II, c. 26—*Opera Omnia*, XVI, 244.

38 Vromant, *De Bonis Ecclesiae Temporalibus*, p. 161, n. 182.

d) buying and selling what is required for the daily maintenance of the religious community;

e) the reparation of damages done to real estate or stable capital;[39]

f) the administration of the money and goods of the community;

g) the acceptance of donations;

h) the leasing of possessions when the rent does not exceed the value of one hundred and sixty dollars provided the lease will not extend beyond a period of nine years.[40]

### ARTICLE 4. THE LOCAL SUPERIOR AND EXTRAORDINARY ADMINISTRATION

Much has already been written on the extraordinary administration of temporal goods of religious houses. However, since the Holy See has issued a number of decrees in recent years which merit study, and since many of these documents have brought substantial modifications to the legislation controlling the temporal administration of religious goods, it seems imperative to discuss the subject. In doing so, the writer will attempt to stress the interpretation of the new documents and avoid repetitions, although some will be inevitable.

It is practically impossible to list every specific administrative act pertaining to temporal goods that can be classified as one of extraordinary administration. The Sacred Congregation of the Propagation of the Faith, however, issued an instruction enumerating the general acts of administration coming under this classification. This enumeration, given for the dioceses of the Netherlands, is as follows:

a) to accept or renounce an inheritance, legacy, donation or foundation;

b) to purchase immovable goods:

c) to sell, exchange, mortgage or divert in any other way from the place for which they were destined, objects of art, historical documents, or other movable property of great importance;

---

39 On this point, however, the constitutions will usually limit the freedom of various administrators to a certain amount of money beyond which the repairs are to be considered as representing acts of extraordinary administration.

40 Cf. can. 1541, § 2, 3°. On this point, the constitutions of the institute might give stricter norms to be followed.

d) to sell, exchange, mortgage or pawn immovable church property or to subject it to any other servitude or burden, or lease it for a period of more than three years;

e) to borrow large sums of money as a (temporary) loan;

f) to build, raze, or rebuild in a new form a church building or to make extraordinary repairs upon them;

g) to establish a cemetery;

h) to enter as a party involved in a lawsuit.[41]

In any contract involving one of the above-mentioned administrative acts, the local administrator (superior or treasurer) must seek the permission of the higher authority designated in the constitutions of his institute. If such weighty administrative acts were left entirely to the discretion of one single administrator, the well-being of the moral person might be endangered. Since every moral person is by nature perpetual,[42] its temporal assets must be safeguarded. The Church, therefore, with that prudence acquired from her long experience in this field, requires the active participation of more than one authority for certain administrative acts in order to assure the permanence and stability of every religious house.[43] The writer will consider in the following pages only the more important acts of extraordinary administration that a local superior and treasurer encounter most often in the exercise of their duties.

### *Section I. Extraordinary Expenses*

Since the ultimate criterion to distinguish between ordinary and extraordinary administration lies in the object and mode of the particular act as determined by the constitutions and by the competent religious authorities, the administrative acts that have been

---

41 S.C. de Prop. Fide, 21 July, 1856—*Fontes,* VII, n. 4841; Cf. Hayes, "Quaestiones practicae circa administrationem bonorum"—*Acta et Documenta,* I, 662.

42 Can. 102, § 1.

43 Vromant, *De Bonis Ecclesiae Temporalibus,* pp. 164-165, n. 186.

withdrawn from the ordinary powers of the local superior are considered as extraordinary.[44] In such cases, canon 1527, § 1 serves as a norm of action for all religious administrators. The canon postulates the permission of a higher authority for the validity of an act of administration whenever the administrator exceeds the end or the mode of ordinary administration.

An expenditure is considered extraordinary whenever the money used in the transaction comes from the stable capital of the religious house or whenever part of free capital is used to buy an object not necessary for the maintenance of personnel and property. Stable capital may be defined as those assets set aside by competent authority in order to remain intact as a permanent asset or as a source of regular income. Money invested by competent authorities likewise is aggregated to the permanent assets of the moral person. However, the revenue accruing from stable capital is at the disposal of the superior for lawful use within the limits established by the constitutions concerning the disposition of such revenue. It may be transferred into the annual income of the house or it may be designated for some other purpose by competent authority, provided it conforms to the accepted mode of administration.

### *Section II. Alienation*

Alienation is an act of extraordinary administration. Therefore, the local superior cannot validly alienate any of the permanent assets belonging to the house without the permission of higher authorities. Modern canonists speak of alienation in two different connotations. In its broad sense, alienation embraces any act by which the right of ownership is transferred, as well as any transaction whereby the *dominium* of property is diminished without necessarily being entirely surrendered.[45] Strictly speaking, alienation implies the transfer

---

[44] "If particular law should establish that permission be sought from the Provincial for all expenditures in excess of a certain amount, the latter amount marks the limit of the ordinary administration."—O'Brien, *The Provincial Religious Superior,* The Catholic University of America Canon Law Series, n. 258 (Washington, D.C.: The Catholic University of America Press, 1947), p. 170.

[45] In the discussion, small gifts and donations to individuals are not included since they are covered by different laws.

of the direct dominion of an object to another. The notion of alienation in canon 534 § 1, however, must be interpreted in the broad connotation.[46] Thus, the laws governing alienation apply to mortgages, leases, long term rentals, loans, passive servitude, surety for others, the contracting of debts, yielding lawsuits, and pawning of religious goods. In each of these instances, the temporal position of the religious house is affected.

Canon 534, § 1 obliges religious superiors to obtain an apostolic indult for acts involving the alienation of religious property whenever the value of the property exceeds the sum of thirty-thousand francs. Much has been written on the true meaning of thirty-thousand francs, and only in 1953 was the matter settled by the Sacred Congregation of Religious. For many years after the promulgation of the Code, many canonists agreed that the sum of thirty-thousand francs was based on the gold standard, and not on paper currency or on other means of exchange.[47] Augustine adhered to the opinion that the value of the thirty-thousand francs was to be computed from the value of actual currency rather than from the gold standard.[48] The Sacred Congregation of Religious, however, in a notice published in 1953 effectively ended any discussion of practical import on the question.[49] It stated that the thirty thousand francs mentioned in canon 534, § 1 was to be no longer regarded as the standard by which to determine when an apostolic indult was necessary for an act of alienation. Henceforth, the permission of the Holy See should be sought by religious in the United States of America whenever the value of the object to be alienated was considered to exceed the sum of five thousand dollars, taken at their current value.

---

[46] Can. 1533.

[47] Ellis, "Triginta millia libellarum seu francorum"—*Periodica,* XXVII (1938), 350; Schaefer, *De Religiosis,* p. 433, n. 204; Doheny, *Practical Problems of Church Finance in the United States* (Milwaukee: Bruce, 1941), p. 41.

[48] Augustine, *A Commentary of the Code of Canon Law,* III, 186.

[49] S.C. de Rel., Notification, 29 Jan., 1953 (Prot. No. 2422/46)—Bouscaren, Canon Law Digest, IV, 203. This notification gives the sums of money, in the actual currency of 20 countries, as the limit beyond which the permission of the Holy See is required according to canon 534, § 1.

Canon 534, § 1 also prohibits the alienation of precious goods without the permission of the Holy See. Pre-Code legislation did not define the notion of precious goods. The constitution *Ambitiosae* mentioned the term without explanation or definition.[50] Pre-Code authors considered as precious all objects pertaining to the treasury of the Church such as chalices, ciboria, sacred vestments of considerable value, as well as rare and artistic objects.[51] The Code of Canon Law defines the term as goods that have a notable value by reason of artistic, historical or material content.[52] Evidently, this definition does not differ substantially from that given by pre-Code authors. The idea still remains vague and subject to diverse interpretations.

If an object has artistic or historical value, as for example, a rare book, a woodcarving, or a painting, it is considered precious regardless of the value of the material. A painting, a sculpture, or a tapestry may be worth very little if its material make-up alone is considered, but its commercial value may be well above that amount due to its artistic content. Likewise, ancient manuscripts, public or private documents, or coins, may be worth thousands of dollars by reason of historical content, although their material value may not be great. In such cases, the problem of distinguishing precious goods from non-precious objects is not too difficult.

Difficulties arise when one considers goods which are precious in view of their material content. When should such goods be considered precious? To date, the Holy See has issued no official document on this question.[53] Some authors, relying on the response of the Sacred Congregation of the Council of 1919[54] maintain that the

---

[50] C. un. *Extra. Comm.*, III, 4.

[51] Bouix, *De Jure Regularium*, II, 285-286; Tamburini, *De Jure Abbatum*, II, disp. XIII, q. I, n. 10-11; Mocchegiani, *Jurisprudentia Ecclesiastica* (3 vols., Rome: 1904), I, p. 641, n. 1289.

[52] Can. 1497.

[53] Coronata, *Institutiones*, II, p. 448, n. 1034; McManus, *The Administration of Temporal Goods in Religious Institutes*, p. 141.

[54] S.C. Conc., Case, 13 July, 1919—*AAS*, XI (1919), 416. This point was proposed directly as an explicit *dubium* to the Sacred Congregation of the Council, which declined to answer. The Congregation referred the *dubium* to

value of one thousand francs or two-hundred dollars constitutes an object of notable value.[55] A second school of authors maintains that a notable value is above five thousand dollars.[56]

From the opinions of these authors, it seems that the precious character of an object in view of its intrinsic worth consists solely in its monetary value.[57] The monetary value, however, should not be the sole factor to be considered. Otherwise, all goods evaluated above this predetermined amount would have to be considered as precious, and this could lead to absurd conclusions as will be seen.

The first condition for an object to be classified as precious by reason of its material content is that it must be made of precious metal or of precious stones.[58] This seems clear from the definitions given by pre-Code authors, who enumerate in their commentaries concerning precious goods only those objects made of valuable material, such as chalices, ciboria, etc.

The second condition is that the object be of notable value. This notable value, however, need not be absolute and applicable to all precious objects, but can be relative. To better understand the relativity of the concept of notable value, a parallel may be drawn between the notable value of a precious object and the sum of money constituting grave matter in questions of justice. At the beginning of

---

the Pontifical Commission for the Interpretation of the Code: S.C. Conc. 14 Jan., 1922—*AAS,* XIV (1922), 160. As yet, no authentic answer to this *dubium* has been issued by the Commission.

55 Huot, *art. cit.—CpRM,* XXXIII (1954), 71; McManus, *The Administration of Temporal Goods in Religious Institutes,* p. 71.

56 Prummer, *Manuale Theologiae Moralis,* II, n. 525; Cerato, *Censurae Vigentes* (Patavii: 1921), n. 43.

57 Schmalzgrueber proposes that a precious object must be worth at least 25 gold pieces; *Jus Ecclesiasticum Universum,* lib. III, tit. 13, n. 33; other authors propose various values; D'Annibale, *Summula Theologiae Moralis,* III, n. 77, note 7; Wernz, *Jus Decretalium,* III, n. 160; Cappello, *De Censuris,* n. 406; Vermeersch, *De Religiosis Institutis et Personis Tractatus Canonico-Moralis ad Recentissimas Leges Exactus* (2 vols., Romae: 1902), I, n. 436.

58 McManus, *The Administration of Temporal Goods in Religious Institutes,* p. 140.

the century, the sum of money constituting grave matter was certainly much less than it is today. Genicot[59] gives in American currency the amount set by certain authors. He mentions that Koning and Sabetti considered one dollar as constituting a notable sum for a farmer, two dollars for a mechanic, two to three dollars for a rich man; also that Sabetti determined five dollars as a sum *absolute gravis,* while Koning required ten dollars. Today, such sums are not considered as constituting grave matter, and one author even lays down as the absolute standard the sum of one hundred dollars.[60] Therefore, if in 1919, a thousand francs or two hundred dollars were considered as a notable value by canonists, it seems that this sum should be raised proportionately in relation to the ever-changing living standards of society, and should vary with the varying conditions to be found in different countries. If the parallel explained above is maintained, the notable value of precious goods should be set at a sum much higher than two-hundred dollars. In the light of this consideration, the opinion of Fanfani and Choupin seems very reasonable. They both maintain that a precious object is one evaluated at ten thousand francs or approximately thirty-three hundred dollars of actual currency.[61] Due to these considerations, it seems probable that a higher sum than two-hundred dollars should be established as *notabilis valor,* notwithstanding the opinion of the great number of authors who uphold the norm of two-hundred dollars. This last sum does not seem considerable enough to require an apostolic indult, since the Church permits the alienation of other goods evaluated at less than five thousand dollars without such an indult.

Moreover, the amount of *notabilis valor* should vary in relation to the nature of the object in question, and in consideration of the circumstances that might affect the preciousness of the object. How then is one to know whether a given object has a notable value or

---

59 Genicot, *Theologiae Moralis Institutiones* (2 vols., 6 ed., Brussells: Dewit, 1909), I, 456, note (2).

60 Jone-Adelman, *Moral Theology* (Westminster: Newman Press, 1956) p. 218, n. 324.

61 Fanfani, *De Jure Religiosorum,* p. 177, n. 158; Choupin, *Nature et Obligations de l'Etat Religieux* (Paris: Beauchesne, 1927), 248.

not? Canon 1530, § 1, 1° seems to provide the answer to this question. This canon states that a written appraisal of property made by trustworthy experts is required before alienation of movable or immovable goods can be permitted. This norm should certainly be applied to precious objects. Since the canon explicitly mentions movable goods, and precious goods are movable, it follows that they are subject to the laws of alienation and must be handled accordingly. However, the appraisal of the experts should take into account not only the pecuniary value of the object, but also its quality as a precious object. Most authors, as it has been noted, maintain that a precious object is one whose value exceeds a specific amount. However, the character of preciousness must not be determined merely in terms of money. Other factors, such as the scarcity of the object, its difficulty of replacement, and the existing economic conditions must also be taken into consideration.

For example, if the monetary value served as the only determining factor, a chalice worth two hundred dollars would be precious. If a local house wished to alienate such a chalice, the superior would have to obtain the previous permission of the Holy See. It is evident that today a chalice of this value is not considered precious, although it could have been so considered in previous years. For this reason, the determining factor in classifying an object as precious should be the decision of the experts. An expert may well judge that the market price of a given object is more than two hundred dollars, and yet that it should not be considered precious.

The formalities that the religious superior must follow whenever he intends to alienate religious property evaluated above five thousand dollars or considered as precious are enumerated in canon 1530. It might be objected that canon 1530 does not apply to the alienation of religious property, since canon 534, § 1 mentions explicitly only canon 1531. Although this objection has some merit, it is nevertheless more logical that religious superiors and officials should be bound by the prescriptions of canon 1530 since these prescriptions form the basis of those laid down in canon 1531. The first paragraph of canon 1531 presupposes that the property to be alienated has been evaluated by experts according to canon 1530, § 1, 1°. Moreover, the new Oriental Code, in parallel places, mentions explicitly the canon in question. Canon 66 of the Oriental Code concerning *De Religiosis,* which is the parallel to canon 534 of the Latin Code, refers explicitly to canon 279 contained under the rubric *De Bonis Ecclesiae Temporalibus.* This latter canon is the parallel of canon 1530 of the Latin Code. Although the Oriental Code does not bind the members of the Latin Church, the parallel between the legislation of both codes nevertheless indicates the importance that the Church attaches to the formalities enumerated in canon 1530.

When the religious superior deems it necessary to start alienation proceedings, he must obtain an appraisal of the property in question by experts. He need not necessarily consult professional appraisers; it is sufficient to call on any individual who is competent to judge the intrinsic value, as well as the market-value, of the object to be alienated. This condition does not affect the validity of the alienation.

The second requirement postulated by canon 1530 is the existence of a just cause. Some pre-Code canonists were of the opinion that the *justa causa* was necessary for the validity of the alienation, but contemporary jurists do not require a just cause for the validity of the act. Modern canonists enumerate three causes that justify an alienation: urgent necessity; evident utility of the Church; and the cause of piety.[62]

Urgent necessity exists when there is no other way to supply a need except by the alienation of property.[63] Alienation is an odious contract in ecclesiastical law and should not be undertaken unless other possibilities have been exhausted. If the necessity is not urgent, the religious authorities should seek some other settlement.

An alienation is undertaken for the evident utility of the Church if it is evidently profitable or advantageous to the Church or to the religious moral person. The word "utility" implies that the Church

---

62 Larraona, "Commentarium Codicis"—*CpR,* XIII (1932), 355.

63 McManus, *The Administration of Temporal Goods in Religious Institutes,* p. 126.

or the religious house will find itself in a better financial situation as a result of the alienation. The simple fact that the religious house will suffer no harm from the contract is not in itself sufficient reason. Also, since the utility must be evident, it necessarily follows that a purely probable, or a *fortiori* a possible, advantage is insufficient.

Piety is the last cause recognized by the Church as adequate to justify an alienation. In this category are included spiritual and corporal works of mercy, the construction of necessary schools, orphanages and hospitals.[64]

Once the religious authorities feel justified in alienating religious property and have been informed of the value of the property, they must then seek the necessary permission from major superiors and possibly from the Holy See. If the property to be alienated has been evaluated by the experts in excess of five thousand dollars, or if a precious object is involved in the contract, their next step must be to obtain the permission of the Holy See.[65] If the object is evaluated at less than five thousand dollars, and if it is not a precious object, the superior need only obtain permission from the legitimate religious superior, as provided for in the constitutions of the institute.[66] The requirement of the canon that the permission be given in writing does not seem necessary for the validity of the permission.[67] This religious superior may be either the superior general, if large sums are involved, or, in cases of lesser sums, the provincial superior. Although recourse to Rome is not required in all cases, the permission either of the Holy See or of the legitimate religious superior is necessary in every case for the validity of alienation. Any provision of civil law legalizing alienations of Church property performed

---

64 Cleary, *Canonical Limitations on the Alienation of Church Property*, The Catholic University of America Canon Law Studies, n. 100 (Washington, D.C.: The Catholic University of America Press, 1936), p. 64.

65 Can. 534, § 1; S.C. de Rel., Notification, 29 Jan., 1953, (Prot. No. 2422/46)—Bouscaren, *Canon Law Digest*, IV, 203.

66 " . . . secus, requiritur et sufficit licentia, in scriptis data, Superioris ad normam constitutionum."—Can. 534, § 1.

67 Coronata, *Institutiones*, I, p. 683, n. 560, note 10.

without previous authorization of one or both of these authorities is devoid of all binding force.[68]

In recent years, the Holy See has granted special faculties to the Apostolic Delegate to the United States and to local Ordinaries concerning the alienation of religious property. In 1946, the Sacred Congregation of Religious granted to the Apostolic Delegate to the United States the fraculty to permit loans and alienations of religious property whose price does not exceed a half-million gold dollars, provided that the norms issued by the Apostolic Delegate in 1936 are faithfully observed.[69] Moreover, the Holy See has recently granted faculties to local Ordinaries to permit, in certain circumstances, the alienation of religious property evaluated at ten thousand American dollars.

> Whenever there is urgent necessity, evident usefulness, and danger in delay, the faculty is granted to permit to all concerned, according to the norms of canons 534, §1 and 1532, § 1, 2° the alienation of ecclesiastical property or property of pious causes whose price does not exceed double the increased amount established in the various Nations by the Sacred Consistorial Congregation in its Notification of 18 October, 1952.[70]

Once the competent religious authorities have fulfilled the prescriptions of canon 1530, § 1, they may then proceed to alienate the religious property in question. Canon 1531 provides the procedure that the authorities should follow. The canon lays down as a general rule that the alienation of ecclesiastical goods should be made by public auction, or at least that the proposed alienation should be publicized.[71] This preceptive obligation, however, admits

---

68 Cf. can. 1529.

69 Apostolic Delegate to the United States, Letter, 3 April, 1947—Bouscaren, *Canon Law Digest,* III, 368.

70 S.C. Consist., private—Bouscaren, *Canon Law Digest,* IV, 73. The notification of 18 October, 1952 may be found in Bouscaren, *Canon Law Digest,* IV, 391.

71 Can. 1531, § 2.

of exceptions; *nisi aliud circumstantiae suadeant.* In the United States, alienation by way of public auction is not customary. Furthermore, even the public advertising of such a sale may not always be the best procedure, since this fact alone may lower the market-value of the property and may occasion serious inconveniences to the religious house. Such a procedure often connotes in the United States a state of bankruptcy and may possibly entail the loss of the good name of the religious house through suspicion of mismanagement. It may be preferable, where these conditions prevail, to proceed through the intermediary of a reliable real-estate agency. In other circumstances, the alienation may even be transacted privately. Fear of being harassed by civil government, danger of public scandal or of lawsuits, taxation, loss of prestige are reasons that may justify a departure from the prescribed course of action.[72] It is the province of the competent religious official who has received the permission to alienate property, to judge when circumstances such as those described above exist, since he is generally in a better position to do so.[73] However, he remains subject to the decisions of the superior granting the permission, who may reserve to himself final judgment on the circumstances which will justify the departure from the prescribed method of procedure.

The object to be alienated must not be sold at a price less than the appraised value.[74] If the experts have agreed on a maximum and minimum value, the latter may be accepted. Quite obviously, more than the maximum value may be accepted, if no injustice is caused. However, if no one is found to offer the appraised price of the object, the competent religious authority may have a new appraisal of the object made to see if, under such circumstances, the original appraisal was not too high.[75]

---

[72] Larraona, "Commentarium Codicis"—*CpR,* XIII (1932), 358.

[73] Larraona, "Commentarium Codicis"—*CpR,* XIII (1932), 358; Cleary, *op. cit.,* p. 68.

[74] Can. 1531, § 1.

[75] McManus, *The Administration of Temporal Goods in Religious Institutes,* pp. 135-136.

The last provision of canon 1531 requires the local superior to invest the money received from the alienation.[76] The proceeds must be used to rebuild the stable capital depleted by the alienation. Therefore, whenever money has been realized from an alienation, the superior is obliged, as a general rule, to place the money in a safe and profitable investment. It cannot be presumed that the cause justifying the alienation will necessarily justify the expenditure of the money received. In order to use these proceeds the permission of the Holy See may be necessary if it is not already implied in the conferral of the indult.[77]

However, in most instances, the reason for the alienation will indicate the use to be made of the proceeds. Usually, the Holy See provides for the use of these proceeds in the formula authorizing the alienation. If, however, the money is to be invested, the proper major superiors must authorize this act since it is one of extraordinary administration.

If the alienation involves an amount less than five thousand dollars, may the religious superior who grants permission for the alienation also grant permission to spend the proceeds of the alienation, or must the local superior have recourse to Rome for such an expenditure? Larraona mentions that the Sacred Congregation of Religious has no formula for granting permission to dispose of the proceeds of alienations permitted by religious superiors for the simple reason that such permissions are never sought.[78] He explains that the superior permitting the alienation is convinced that he may also grant permission to spend the money effected by the alienation. The superior who grants the permission to alienate may also permit the expenditure of the proceeds for the reason that the cause justifying the alienation usually requires this expenditure.[79] However, if there is no need for the expenditure, the local superior must invest the proceeds for the benefit of the religious house prudently, safely and fruitfully.[80]

---

[76] Can. 1531, § 3.

[77] S.C. Conc., Case, 13 July, 1919—Bouscaren, *Canon Law Digest,* I, 728.

[78] Larraona, "Commentarium Codicis"—*CpR,* XIII (1932), 360.

[79] Larraona, "Commentarium Codicis"—*CpR,* XIII (1932), 361.

[80] Larraona, "Commentarium Codicis"—*CpR,* XIII (1932), 361.

As a general rule, the aforesaid solemnities bind every local religious superior whenever he wishes to sell part of the stable property of the religious house to another person, be it physical or moral, ecclesiastical or civil. Certain authors, however, have probed further into this problem, particularly in reference to alienations between religious houses of the same institute. Some hold that in certain congregations alienations in cases involving property evaluated at more than five thousand dollars may be performed without the previous consent of the Holy See.[81] Bastient maintains the contrary opinion.[82]

Authors argue that if the constitutions deny the right of ownership to local houses according to canon 531, and state that only the institute may own property, and that in these cases the stable property remains in the hands of the same moral person, i.e. of the institute, and the alienation effects a change in the locality of the property and not a transfer of the *dominium,* it is clear that the prescriptions of canon 534, § 1 are not binding.[83]

Larraona further states as his belief that, whenever the constitutions are silent on the right to property of local houses, the permission of the Holy See is not required for alienations beyond five thousand dollars between two local houses of centralized institutes.[84] A centralized institute, as understood here, is opposed to a monastic Order of individual monasteries *sui juris* and consists in a congregation whose government is centered in some way in a superior general. Most modern religious communities are considered as centralized institutes. Whenever two moral persons of such institutes are the parties of an alienation, whether they be two local houses, a house and a province, or a house and the institute, they are not obliged to

---

81 "Leges alienationis non tenent, uti videtur, inter diversas ejusdem Religionis personas morales."—Schaefer, *De Religiosis,* p. 430, n. 201; Huot,

82 "Les aliénations entre maisons religieuses ne nous paraissent pas permises sans les formalités requises par la loi ecclésiastique."—*Directoire Canonique, art. cit.—CpRM,* XXXIV (1955), 269; Larraona, "Commentarium Codicis"—*CpR,* XIII (1932), 187-188.

p. 244, n. 365.

83 Larraona, "Commentarium Codicis"—*CpR,* XIII (1932), 187.

84 *Ibid.,* pp. 187-188.

have recourse to the Holy See. Vromant admits the principle of Larraona, but he requires a certain subordination between the two contracting moral persons. He maintains that such alienations may be effected between the institute and a province or a local house, or between the province and a local house, but does not admit that it can take place between two local religious houses without first obtaining the permission of the Holy See.[85]

Larraona justifies his stand by saying that, although the constitutions do not declare the community of goods in the institute, the bonds that unite together the moral persons of the same institute remove the juridical character of economic negotiations. It is a common feeling among religious that such contracts between two moral persons of the same institute be not as rigidly regulated as contracts involving persons outside the institute. Larraona adds that permission for such alienations are never sought. These transactions are regulated by the constitutions which have been approved by the Holy See, and which often permit such contracts without permission from Rome.[86] However, alienations between two local religious houses of non-centralized institutes remain subject to the canon 534, § 1, so that for every alienation between such moral persons above the amount of five thousand dollars, the *beneplacitum* of the Holy See is required.

### *Section III. Debts*

The legislation concerning the alienation of religious property is also applicable whenever a local superior intends to incur debts that will endanger the condition of the stable capital of the religious house. Canon 534, § 1 is clear in stating that to incur a debt for a sum beyond thirty thousand francs, a special indult of the Holy See is necessary for the validity of the act.[87] For the contracting of debts less than that requiring an apostolic indult, the particular law of

---

85 Vromant, *De Bonis Ecclesiae Temporalibus*, p. 275, n. 325.

86 Larraona, "Commentarium Codicis"—*CpR*, XIII (1932), 188.

87 The sum of thirty thousand francs has been reduced for the United States to a sum of five thousand dollars. Cf. *supra*, p. 67.

each institute must be scrupulously observed. The canonical legislation concerning the incurrence of debts by religious superiors has been well explained in a letter of the Apostolic Delegate to the United States sent to every religious superior in 1936.[88]

A problem has arisen concerning the coalescence of debts. Must the local superior of a religious house, already indebted for four thousand dollars, have recourse to Rome before incurring an additional debt of two thousand dollars? Further, if a religious house is already indebted for six thousand dollars, must it obtain the *beneplacitum* of the Holy See for all subsequent debts no matter what the amount of the debt may be? The opinion of canonists seems to differ from the norms to be followed by the religious superiors in the United States. Canonists seem to agree that such debts do not coalesce if the superior or the procurator who incurs the debt does not act *in fraudem legis* and if the debts are incurred separately and with no moral unity.[89] Therefore, if a local house is already indebted to the amount of four thousand dollars, and later intends to incur a debt of two thousand dollars, the *beneplacitum* of the Holy See is not necessary provided that the second debt was not foreseen at the time of the incurrence of the first debt.

> When a community contracts several debts within a short space of time, these acts become morally one. Hence, the authorization of the Holy See is required to accept two loans at short intervals, e. g. one for four thousand dollars and the other for two thousand dollars. But if the acts are sufficiently separated in time and when in good faith, one has not foreseen the need of the second loan at the time the first loan was accepted, there would seem no need of adding the two sums together and considering them as one.[90]

---

[88] Apostolic Delegate to the United States, Letter, 13 Nov., 1936—Bouscaren, *Canon Law Digest*, II, 161-165.

[89] Goyeneche, *Quaestiones Canonicae De Jure Religiosorum*, I, 249; Creusen-Ellis, *Religious Men and Women in the Code* (Milwaukee: Bruce, 1940), p. 122; Vermeersch-Creusen, *Epitome*, I, p. 474, n. 658.

[90] Creusen-Ellis, *Religious Men and Women in the Code*, p. 123.

This interpretation by the majority of canonists is certainly well supported by canon 534, § 1. If the canon is examined closely, it becomes clear that the *beneplacitum* of the Holy See is required only when the debt to be incurred is beyond thirty thousand francs. The text of the canon makes no reference whatsoever to debts already incurred in the past. Therefore, each debt is considered separately, and has no relation to past debts. If the legislator had intended to include past debts in the evaluation of the thirty thousand francs, he would have mentioned them explicitly as he did in the Instruction *Inter Ea.*[91]

However, the letter of the Apostolic Delegate to the United States, sent to religious superiors of the United States, provides the following norms which are in perfect accordance with the prescriptions of the Instruction *Inter Ea.*

> An apostolic indult is required not only in the event of a single transaction exceeding the sum of six thousand dollars, but an apostolic indult is necessary in every case where a coalescence of the debts or obligations of every kind and nature exceeds the said sum of six thousand dollars. For example:
>
> 1. If after having contracted a loan of four thousand dollars, an occasion arises for borrowing a further sum of more than two thousand dollars before payment of the first has been made by the religious—since the total of the financial obligations will exceed six thousand dollars after the second borrowing, it is necessary to have the permission of the Holy See before incurring the second loan . . .
>
> 4. When the amount of *existing* debts or obligations totals four thousand dollars and it is proposed to increase such total indebtedness to more than six thousand dollars, then an apostolic indult is necessary. And such permission is required whether the proposed increase in indebtedness is by contract, mortgage, bond, or debenture issue, or any

---

[91] *Inter Ea,* art III.

other form which will bring the actual or contingent obligation to a *total sum* of more than six thousand dollars.
5. When the total *present indebtedness* is over six thousand dollars, an apostolic indult is required for any contract, debt, or other obligation, even if such new indebtedness is incurred for the purpose of complete or partial payment of the pre-existing debts or obligations.[92]

This Letter of the Apostolic Delegate does not make absolutely clear whether these prescriptions constitute an interpretation of a doubtful law, or whether they give an extensive interpretation, or whether they are additional norms prescribed to ensure a better observance of canon 534, § 2 and a greater prudence on the part of religious superiors in financial transactions. In any case, since this Letter was issued by the Apostolic Delegate with the authorization of the Sacred Congregation of Religious, these prescriptions bind every religious superior in the United States.[93] As for religious superiors outside the United States, it seems that the opinion of modern canonists may be followed, at least until the Holy See deems it opportune to issue further instructions on this matter.

In the petition sent to the Holy See, the religious superior must provide the following information: the reason for contracting the debt; the nature of the debt or obligation; the name of the person or firm with whom the debt is to be contracted and the proposed terms for meeting the debt or obligation. The local superior must, therefore, provide the higher authorities with the elements, facts, and considerations necessary to enable the superiors granting the permission to pass an objective judgment on the matter. Thus, it is insufficient to indicate in a general way the nature of the transaction and the sum of money involved; the religious superior must also

92 Apostolic Delegate to the United States, Letter, 13 Nov., 1936—Bouscaren, *Canon Law Digest,* II, 163-164. The sum of six thousand dollars mentioned in this Letter has now been reduced to five thousand dollars in accord with the Notification of the Sacred Congregation of Religious of January 29, 1953; cf. S.C. de Rel., Replies (Prot. N. 2422/46)—Bouscaren, *Canon Law Digest,* IV, 203.

93 Bouscaren, *Canon Law Digest,* IV, 204-205.

specify the conditions and the motives, state the resources at his disposal or on which he can count, in order to meet the further expenses and obligations incurred. Without this information, a permission granted by a higher authority would be reduced to a mere formality, to a mere vote of confidence, and would in no wise be an effective control of the administration.[94]

### *Section IV. Debentures and Annuities*

The local superior ought to have a clear notion of the meaning of and the legislation concerning debentures and annuities. A debenture is any legally recognized certificate serving as evidence of a debt, or of a right to demand a certain amount of money. An annuity, on the other hand, is a "bilateral contract whereby one party agrees to pay another a fixed sum at specific periods in return for a gross amount of money or equivalent received".[95] The annuity may be *contingent* if it covers only an undetermined number of years; v.g. until the annuitant marries; *certain* if it covers a predetermined number of years, v.g. until the annuitant reaches the age of sixty; and life annuity, if the annuity is to cease with the death of the annuitant.

The local superior must consult his constitutions whenever he wishes to enter such contracts. The general legislation of the Church concerning these two classes of contracts has been explained in the letter of the Apostolic Delegate to the United States in 1936.

> An apostolic indult is required . . . if a community undertakes several issues of bonds or debentures, each being within the limit permitted by Canon Law, but the total of the issues aggregating a sum exceeding six thousand dollars . . . In the event that a community desires to obtain money by means of *annuities* or life pensions, there will be no need of

---

[94] Apostolic Delegate to the United States, 13 Nov., 1936—Bouscaren, *Canon Law Digest*, II, 164-165.

[95] Heston, *The Alienation of Church Property in the United States*, The Catholic University of America Canon Law Studies, n. 132 (Washington, D.C.: The Catholic University of America Press, 1941), p. 68.

> recourse to the Holy See for a sum up to six thousand dollars, but when the sums aggregate a sum exceeding six thousand dollars, then the community cannot receive any further funds through such annuities without an apostolic indult.[96]

When a religious house undertakes several issues of bonds or debentures, an apostolic indult is necessary when the total of all the issues exceeds the sum of five thousand dollars. If a religious house has received money or property to the value of five thousand dollars under annuity agreements, no further money or property may be accepted under this system without an apostolic indult. Moreover, the local superior may not carry out any further transaction without an indult from the Holy See when the funds accepted under either or both of the systems mentioned total five thousand dollars. If the sum of money involved in either or both of these systems, added to other outstanding debts or obligations, totals beyond five thousand dollars, an apostolic indult is necessary to make further transactions.[97]

These prescriptions were approved by the Sacred Congregation of Religious as late as 1955 and were further explained in a letter of this Sacred Congregation to the Apostolic Delegate to the United States. It was asked whether the permission of the Holy See is required "whenever the total amount which is the object of the 'annuities' contract exceeds the value of 30,000 francs, or rather whenever the sum to be paid annually by the moral person to the benefactor exceeds the value of 30,000 francs?" The Congregation answered in the affirmative to the first part and in the negative to the second part.[98]

---

96 Apostolic Delegate to the United States, Letter, 13 Nov., 1936—Bouscaren, *Canon Law Digest,* II, 163-165. Evidently, in this text, the sum of six thousand dollars is the equivalent of five thousand dollars of actual currency; cf. Bouscaren, *Canon Law Digest,* IV, 203.

97 Apostolic Delegate to the United States, Letter, 13 Nov., 1936—Bouscaren, *Canon Law Digest,* II, 163-164.

98 Bouscaren, *Canon Law Digest,* IV, 204-206.

### *Section V. Gratuities*

Under the present legislation, the local superiors are permitted to make gifts and donations provided that they are made according to the prescriptions of the constitutions of the institute. If the gift or gratuity assumes large proportions, the constitutions or particular statutes or custom will probably require the local superior to obtain the consent of his council or even of his provincial. If the gift is made from the stable capital of the religious house, it would constitute an alienation, and therefore would require the fulfillment of the canonical regulations of canon 534.

In conclusion, it must be added that the competent superiors must obtain the consent of their council for the alienation of any property evaluated at less than five thousand dollars unless the value in such a case is left to the discretion of the superior alone.[99] Without this consent, the alienation would be invalid since canon 105, 1° is operative in such cases. The secrecy of the ballot and the requirement that the permission of the superior be given in writing are not considered as necessary for the validity. For all other acts of extraordinary administration, particular law and custom will provide the norms that the local superiors must follow.

## ARTICLE 5. THE LOCAL SUPERIOR AND NON-RELIGIOUS PROPERTY

The religious of clerical congregations may be entrusted with the care and administration of parishes. Therefore, the problem arises concerning the rights of the local superior over the non-religious property of the parish. Canon 630 supposes that religious of clerical institutes may be put in charge of two kinds of parishes; a secular parish, not united to the religious house, but committed to its care with permission of the Holy See according to canon 626, § 1, and a parish united *pleno jure* or incorporated with the religious house according to canon 1425, § 2.

Since the property of a secular parish does not belong to the local religious house, the administration of such property is subject to the

[99] Can. 534, § 1.

jurisdiction of the local Ordinary and must be carried out according to the norms of canons 1495-1551 and the particular legislation of the diocese. To administer such non-religious property, the religious superior presents a priest of his community to the Ordinary of the place and the latter appoints the candidate according to canon 459, § 2.[100] The religious administrator, however, must not be considered as released from all religious authority. Frequently, the pastor of the parish is also named superior of the local house and is invested with the power of both pastor and local religious superior. In such cases, he remains subject to the vigilance of his major religious superiors, even as administrator of the parish. It often happens, however, that the pastor is distinct from the local superior. In such a case, the religious pastor is subject to both the local and major superiors. In both cases, the religious pastor remains subject to the prescriptions of his constitutions insofar as their observance is compatible with the exercise of his function as pastor.[101] This article will attempt to determine the nature and extent of the power of vigilance of religious superiors over the administration of non-religious property as mentioned in canon 630, § 4.

The meaning of vigilance has been defined differently by various authors, and therefore needs some explanation. Vigilance is a broad but not a vague term. It is used no less than forty-eight times in the Code; thirty times it refers to the powers of the local Ordinary, and twice to the penal remedy of vigilance.[102] Vigilance, as distinguished from administration of temporal goods, consists in the right to be informed, either *per se* or *per alios,* of the amount and worth of goods; the right to demand an account of the investments and faithful application of donations; and also the right to prescribe that the administration be orderly and according to law.[103] It does not include, however, the right to determine the manner in which the income and donations are to be spent, nor to reserve to oneself the entire distribution or the partial outlay of these goods. This right

---

100 Can. 456.

101 Can. 630, § 1.

102 Carew, *The Apostolic Delegate,* The University of Ottawa Canon Law Series, n. 32 (Ottawa, Ontario: The University of Ottawa, 1950), p. 41. (MS)

103 Vromant, *De Bonis Ecclesiae Temporalibus,* p. 163, n. 184.

belongs exclusively to the administrator upon whom devolves the immediate duty of administration.[104]

To be truly effective, such vigilance over the administration of non-religious property should not be merely concomitant or subsequent, but must also be *preventive*. Before undertaking any transaction of an extraordinary nature, the religious pastor or administrator of non-religious property must obtain the consent of the local Ordinary. In addition, he must also consult his local or major superior to obtain authorization from him. This authorization is not essentially a mandate nor a permission, but a simple *nihil obstat* which simply shows that the superior does not object to the administrative acts contemplated by the religious pastor. If the religious superior has certain objections to the projects, the matter should be discussed and settled on a local or provincial level before approaching the Ordinary. It would appear that the *nihil obstat* is not necessary for the validity of the act, but is only a precaution to keep the activities of religious administrators within the supervision of their religious superiors.[105]

Canon 630, § 4 clearly gives the extent of the power of the religious superior over the different acts of administration of non-religious property performed by his religious subjects. Notwithstanding his vow of poverty, the religious pastor may gather and receive alms destined for the good of his parishioners or for Catholic schools or for pious institutions connected with the parish. He may also administer alms according to his prudent judgment, always keeping in mind the wishes of the donor. In all these transactions, the religious pastor is subject to the vigilance of the superior. The pastor is the administrator of the goods of the parish and he may within the scope of authority granted him as pastor dispose of them as he sees fit, according to the needs of the parish. The religious superior has no authority other than that of vigilance over the activity of his subject.[106] Therefore, the pastor is not obliged to ask the permission of the superior for such activities, nor can the superior forbid them.

---

104 McManus, *The Administration of Temporal Goods in Religious Institutes*, p. 88.

105 Dailey, *The Primary Effects of the Union Pleno Jure of Parishes with Religious Communities* (Rome: Catholic Book Agency, 1951), p. 45.

106 Dailey, *op. cit.*, pp. 43-44.

# CHAPTER IV

## The Local Treasurer and the Superior of the Religious House

Canon 516, § 2 urges that an econome be named to administer the temporalities of each local religious house. This official is known as the treasurer, the procurator, the bursar or the econome. Reference to a local treasurer is found in the writings of Fagnanus.[1] Following the opinion of Hostiensis, Fagnanus believed that the abbot should not be burdened with the direction of the temporal affairs of the monastery. Clement VIII (1592-1605)[2], in his decree nullus omnino, stated that the burden of administering the temporalities of a house should be assumed by three minor officials. The Council of Trent stated that "the administration of the properties of the monasteries or convents shall belong only to the officials thereof, who are removable at the will of their superiors."[3]

The next really significant pronouncements on this question were made by the Sacred Congregation of Bishops and Regulars, in accordance with the Tridentine norms. They issued a set of *Normae* on June 28, 1901, in which it is clearly stated that the administration of every religious house should be confided to a local treasurer who should exercise his function under the control and direction of the superior and under the vigilance of the local council.[4] In matters pertaining to the administration of the house, the council should require the procurator to provide the necessary documents on which

---

1 Fagnanus, *Commentaria in Quinque Libros Decretalium* (5 vols., Colonia Allobrogum, (1759), ad c. 2, X, *de statu monachorum et canonicorum regularium,* III, 35, n. 74.

2 Clement VIII, decree "Nullus Omnino", 25 July, 1599—*Bullarum Diplomatum et Privilegiorum Romanorum Pontificum Taurinensis Editio,* X, 644; Vermeersch, *De Religiosis* (2 vols., Vol. I, Bruges, 1902, Vol. II, 3 ed., Bruges, 1904), II, 309.

3 C. of Trent, sess. XXV, *de regularibus,* c. 2—Schroeder, *Canons and Decrees,* p. 218.

4 *Normae* of 1901, art. 293.

the legal rights of the moral person are based and to present his opinion on administrative matters. The *Normae* further stated that the superior and members of the council receive from the procurator an account of his administration at least once every six months. They must inspect the books, the property titles, the bank account, the debts and obligations; in a word, everything that pertains to the administration of the local house.[5]

The Code of Canon Law prescribes that each religious house should have a treasurer who is to exercise his office under the direction of the superior.[6] This official thus relieves the superior of the burden of temporal administration and allows him a greater opportunity to attend to the spiritual needs of the community. The Code declares outright that a superior may discharge the office of local bursar if necessity requires it, though it is better to keep this office distinct from that of the superior.[7] The intention of the Code indicates clearly the desirability of both offices being filled by distinct persons, although in cases of necessity, they may be exercised by the same religious. The superior may properly perform the duties of the treasurer if the latter is temporarily incapacitated. Yet, even in such cases, it is preferable that a religious other than the superior should be named to relieve the procurator, especially in the case of a prolonged absence.[8]

The constitutions of each institute usually indicate the procedure that must be followed in the appointment of the local treasurer. However, if the constitutions are silent on this matter, the Code prescribes that this officer be appointed by the major superior with the consent of his council.[9]

The office of the local procurator or treasurer may be defined as that of an official of a local religious house entrusted with the administration of the temporal goods of the local house, in accordance with the constitutions of the institute. His designation as an

---

[5] *Normae* of 1901, art. 293.

[6] Can. 516, § 2.

[7] Can. 516, § 3.

[8] Clancy, *The Local Religious Superior*, p. 70.

[9] Can. 516, § 4.

"official" excludes the attributes of a superior. A local superior is placed in charge of the government of the local house in regard to persons and things, with dominative power recognized by law.[10] The treasurer, however, is not entrusted with the government of the house but is only commissioned to administer the temporalities. Canon 532, § 2 defines the limits of the office of the local treasurer whom it designates as one of the *officiales . . . qui in constitutionibus ad hoc designantur.* His sphere of action is limited to the administration of temporal goods and his power does not extend beyond the range of such administration. He has no dominative power nor any strict power of government.

His duties, nevertheless, are manifold, having many different purposes in regard to the property of the local religious house. The following acts of administration are considered within the scope of his power: the preservation of property and its improvement; the reparation of damages; the exploitation of productive property, the payment of rents and dues. Most of these operations belong to the ordinary administration (see chapter III). Nevertheless, certain of these acts could be classified as extraordinary by the constitutions and therefore necessitate the permission of a superior, either of his own local superior or that of a major superior depending on the constitutions.[11]

In the performance of his administrative functions, the local treasurer is not autonomous but is radically and completely subordinate. The second paragraph of canon 516 states that the local treasurer must exercise the functions of his office under the direction of the superior. In meeting the demands of his office, therefore, the superior is obliged to supervise with care the administration carried out by the local bursar. He must prevent any abuse of power by the procurator. The words *sub directione Superioris* not only grant the superior the right to direct the administration of the local procurator with counsels and exhortations, but also clearly empower him to surpervise, command, and, if need be, to coerce the

---

[10] Can. 501, § 1.

[11] Clancy, *The Local Religious Superior,* pp. 69-71.

procurator in every phase of his administration.[12] A religious house is not directed nor governed by two superiors, one for temporal matters, and another for its spiritual needs. The superior is the only official who possesses dominative power and who is entrusted with the immediate government of the house. The procurator is merely an official who must exercise the powers of his office under the supervision and direction of the superior. Even the acts of ordinary administration performed by the treasurer are subject to the direction of the superior. If the superior objects to the performance of such acts, the treasurer may not posit them. In carrying out acts of extraordinary administration, the treasurer is bound to obey the prescriptions of his constitutions and the directive norms of his superiors governing these acts, and to procure the necessary permissions from the legitimate superiors before performing them.

An endeavor must be made to appoint as treasurers only able and reliable religious of prudent judgment who will submit readily to the prescriptions of the Code and of their own particular constitutions. Since the moral person is often held responsible for the imprudent administration of the local procurators, it is only reasonable that great care be exercised in the nominations to such a position.

The Code provides the general norms that must be followed concerning the responsibility of the religious moral person for the administrative acts of the procurator. Whenever the procurator performs an act of ordinary administration, the religious house alone is responsible provided that such acts are valid. Again, the procurator is not to be held responsible for acts of extraordinary administration performed with the necessary permission of the legitimate superiors.[13]

Reiffenstuel has shed further light on this problem of the responsibility of the moral persons for the administrative acts of the treasurer. He explains that if a treasurer should violate the laws governing

---

[12] *Sanctae Romanae Rotae Decisiones seu Sententiae quae . . . prodierunt anno 1909* (Romae: Typis Vaticanis, 1912—) XXIX (1937), dec. XLVI, p. 453.

[13] Can. 536, §§ 2, 3.

the discharge of his office or should violate the precepts of his superiors, no presumption is created that he was acting as a private individual, nor is the moral person *ipso facto* free of obligation in the eyes of the law. Damages caused by the treasurer are imputed to the moral person if it is proved that an incompetent religious has been named to that office, or supervision over his acts has been neglected. The reasons for this are, according to Reiffenstuel, first to insure that everyone concerned be clearly warned not to permit any damage to be caused to others by his own or his subjects' wrongful acts; secondly, to prevent innumerable frauds and wrongdoings which would be difficult to prove in the external forum.[14] In such cases the local superior himself is not personally obliged to answer for the damages caused by the procurator. Although the superior is responsible in some way for the damages due to lack of supervision, the moral person is nevertheless obliged to compensate for them. The rule of law *delictum personae non debet in detrimentum Ecclesiae redundare,*[15] does not apply in this case. In his commentary, on this rule of law, Reiffenstuel mentions four exceptions to the rule, one of which is the delict of omission.[16] Although the necessary vigilance over the administration of the local procurator is not exercised, the superior is not held responsible for the debts or obligations incurred invalidly by the procurator. Since the superior is the official representative of the local religious house and is responsible in some way for this omission, the moral person must answer for all the juridical consequences of the financial mistakes of the local treasurer.[17]

---

[14] "Partim ut quilibet invigilet amplius, ne sua vel *suorum* culpa damnum aliquod proximis inferatur, sicque pax communis, et publica tranquillitas conservetur; partim ut praecaveatur innumeris fraudibus et malitiis hominum, quae in foro externo sunt difficilioris probationis." Reiffenstuel, lib. V, tit. 36, *de injuriis et damno dato,* n. 44; cf. *Sanctae Romanae Rotae Decisiones seu Sententiae,* XXIX (1937), dec. XLVI, 459-460.

[15] Reg. 76, R.J., in VI°.

[16] "Quaeritur: an et quas fallentias patiatur regula 76. Resp. eam fallere primo in delictis omissionis a praelato, vel aliis personis factis; haec siquidem etiam Ecclesiae praejudicant *arg. can. Placuit* 15, *can.* 16, q. 3. Item, c. I *et seqq. de Praescrip.* ex quibus clare patet, quod delictum praelati, omittentis repetere rem ecclesiasticam, noceat Ecclesiae eatenus, quatenus contra eundem debito tempore currit praescriptio." Reiffenstuel, in Reg. 76, n. 6.

[17] Cf. *Sanctae Romanae Rotae Decisiones seu Sententiae,* XXIX (1937), dec. XLVI, 460.

Although this doctrine regarding the responsibility of the local superior and of the moral person for the administrative acts of the local treasurer is not explicitly mentioned in the Code, it is based nevertheless on the general principles of law,[18] and is in complete harmony with the canonical jurisprudence and with the common teachings of cannonists.[19]

The entire question of the responsibility of the local superior for the administrative acts of the procurator may be summarized thus: 1) the local superior may never be held personally responsible for debts incurred invalidly by the procurator; 2) if the damages are caused in the performance of acts of ordinary administration or in making contracts with the permission of the legitimate superior, the moral person is held responsible and must repair such damages; 3) if the procurator has caused damages during the exercise of his office, but against the prescriptions of law and without the permissions of the legitimate superiors, the local house is held responsible when the superior has neglected his duty of supervision or has knowingly named an incompetent man to the post; 4) the individual procurator will be held personally responsible for damages caused during the exercise of his office only if he has performed administrative acts against the prescriptions of law, and in spite of the vigilance of his superiors.[20]

This severe legislation concerning the responsibility of the religious house in regard to obligations incurred by the local procurator is understandable when one considers that a procurator is generally presumed to be acting in the name of the community. The presumption is that negotiations are conducted with a procurator, not as a private person but always as a representative of the religious house.

---

[18] Can. 20.

[19] *Sanctae Romanae Rotae Decisiones seu Sententiae,* XXIX (1937), XLVI, 457-458.

[20] *Sanctae Romanae Rotae Decisiones seu Sententiae,* XXIX (1937), dec. XLVI, 456-457.

# CHAPTER V

## Major Superiors and The Administration of Local Houses

### Article 1. Major Superiors and the Ordinary Administration of Local Houses

To assure a prudent administration in temporal affairs, the Code establishes a hierarchy of superiors who are responsible for the management of the goods of a religious house. The superior general of the congregation is endowed with supreme power over every religious house of his institute, and this power is to be exercised according to the common law of the Church and the statutes of the particular constitutions.[1] On the next level, the provincial superior exercises a right of vigilance and, at times, of immediate control over the individual houses within the limits of his jurisdiction.[2] At the lowest level, the administration of a local house is entrusted to a local superior, who exercises immediate control over every phase of ordinary administration. The Code provides the office of a local treasurer who must discharge the functions of his office under the direction of the local superior.[3] This plurality of administrators assures a greater security in the administration of temporal goods and a greater prudence in every transaction. In addition, it protects the local moral person from any arbitrary decisions of its administrators. For these reasons, the Code prescribes that permission of certain superiors be sought and obtained before certain administrative acts may be posited. This permission may be required for the liceity of the act or for its validity as in the case of extraordinary administration.[4]

---

1 Can. 502.
2 Can. 502.
3 Cans. 516, § 2, 532, § 2.
4 Vromant, *De Bonis Ecclesiae Temporalibus*, p. 164, n. 186.

In the exercise of his authority, each superior must remain within the scope of his juridical powers. No superior, even though he be a major superior, may interfere with the administration of local houses, except in the cases stipulated by the common law of the code and by the particular constitutions.[5] The law of the Code[6] explicitly gives to local houses a separate right of ownership, apart from that of the institute and province, unless particular law limits this right. Therefore, neither the general nor the provincial superior may dispose of the goods of a particular house without the consent of the local superior and of his council, unless the contratry is stipulated either implicitly or explicitly in the Code of Canon Law or in the particular law of the institute. In certain congregations a more extensive power is granted to the superior general, as will be seen below; but, in the light of the law of the Code alone, as a general rule, it must be maintained that neither the superior general nor the provincial superior may, without the free consent of the interested parties, dispose of property of subordinates without incurring the guilt of injustice.

By the nature of their office, major superiors enjoy a right of supervision over the ordinary administration performed by the superior and officials of a local house. This right is one of vigilance only and not one of administration. Vigilance, as has been said, consists in the right to be informed, either *per se* or *per alios,* of the amount and worth of property; the right to demand an account of the investments and the faithful application of donations; and also the right to prescribe that the administration be orderly and according to law.[7] It does not give the right to the major superior to determine the manner in which the income and donations are to be spent, nor to reserve to himself the entire distribution or the partial outlay of the goods. This right belongs exclusively to the administrator upon whom devolves the immediate duty of administration.[8]

---

[5] Heston, "Some Aspects of Government in Religious Communities"—*The Jurist,* X (1950), 40.

[6] C. 531

[7] Cf. *supra* p. 85.

[8] McManus, *The Administration of Temporal Goods in Religious Institutes,* p. 88.

Since the acts of ordinary administration constitute a stable order of economic activities, which has the general approval of the competent authority, the superior and treasurer may perform such acts without special permission for each particular case. The general approbation of these acts is given by the major superiors either explicitly or implicitly. Consequently, the right of immediate control over these acts belongs to the local superior. The major superiors may supervise the administration of the local superior only to prevent abuse of power, since each house is a moral person with its own rights of administration. Thus, within the limits of ordinary administration, both the local superior and the local procurator act validly and independently of the major superior.[9]

## ARTICLE 2. MAJOR SUPERIORS AND THE EXTRAORDINARY ADMINISTRATION OF LOCAL HOUSES

Besides enjoying the right of vigilance over every act of ordinary administration of local houses, the major superiors also have a right of immediate control over matters of extraordinary administration. Local superiors have no general authorization to perform acts of extraordinary administration.[10] Such acts have been withdrawn from their competence and remain subject to the immediate control of the major superiors. The scope of this right of major superiors will be determined by the particular law of the institute. The constitutions may well establish that permission be sought by the local superior and treasurer for all expenses in excess of a determined amount. This amount then marks the limits of ordinary administration, and all expenses beyond this amount are subject to the control of the competent major superiors.

However, this right of immediate control has some limits. The right of immediate control of the provincial superior is limited by his obligation to have recourse to the superior general in cases determined by the constitutions. Similarly, the right of immediate control of both the provincial and superior general is restricted by their

---

[9] Can. 532, § 2.
[10] Cf. chapter III, 52-54.

obligation to obtain an apostolic indult in cases of alienation involving an amount above five thousand dollars. Canon 534, § 1 lays down the norm to be followed in such cases. The particular constitutions, however, will determine more precisely the prescriptions of this canon, specifying which major superior is competent to grant the permission in these cases, and which councils must be heard before the granting of the permission.

To summarize, it may be said that the duties of the major superiors in relation to the administration of temporal goods of local houses are the following: a) supervision over the ordinary administration in all its phases; b) supervision and immediate control, in virtue of the constitutions, over the extraordinary administration as determined in particular law; c) supervision and immediate control over matters involving alienation both when an apostolic indult is necessary, and, ordinarily under particular law, when such an indult is not needed.[11]

### ARTICLE 3. MAJOR SUPERIORS AND THE RIGHT TO LEVY TAXES

Although local religious houses may have the right to own property, they do not enjoy unrestricted autonomy in the field of temporal administration. The *Normae* of 1901 stated that "every house with a surplus will surrender at the end of each year a third of its annual surplus to the Provincial, after having deducted all of its expenses."[12] This provision of the *Normae* is not mentioned in the Code itself, but since every religious community was obliged to adapt its constitutions to the *Normae,* the particular law of each institute of simple vows usually requires local houses to give part of their annual surplus to the province. In recent years, however, the Sacred Congregation of Religious, in approving the constitutions of religious institutes, permits the general chapter or major superiors to determine the percentage of the annual surplus which must be turned over to the province. This appears to be a better system than the one issued in the *Normae* which proposed a predetermined percentage for all

---

[11] Cf. O'Brien, *The Provincial Religious Superior,* pp. 171-172.
[12] *Normae* of 1901, n. 294.

religious houses, regardless of their individual economic conditions. The general chapter or the major superiors should endeavor to accommodate the amount of the annual tax to the economic potential of each local house. A fixed tax that may easily be paid by one local house could prove harmful to another house in a less fortunate economic condition.[13]

Moreover, major superiors are not justified in compelling the local houses under their jurisdiction to remit their entire annual surplus, unless the constitutions grant them such a right. Such a demand against the accumulation of reserve funds would run counter to the practice of the Holy See, since the Sacred Congregation of Religious rarely approves in the constitutions of religious institutes the stipulation obliging local houses or provinces to remit their entire annual surplus to the common treasury of the province or of the community.[14] Such practice would violate the relative autonomy of the local houses in their administrative rights conceded by the Code and would endanger the security of the local houses by obliging them to share the financial risks of the province or of the institute. Furthermore, the intention of certain donors who wish to endow certain works of the community might be violated. Finally, such a procedure might be opposed to the best interests of the province and the congregation in general. Since religious superiors and treasurers of the local houses are interested in the expansion and development of the field of activity to which each is assigned, it would be inequitable for the fruits of their efforts to be removed in their entirety for some other use, no matter how deserving it might be in itself.[15]

Morever, the questionnaire of the quinquennial report that the superior general must present to the Holy See makes reference to this very question of the annual tax on the surplus of local houses;

---

13 Fernandez, "Bona Religiosa Societatum sine votis et Institutum Saecularium"—*Acta et Documenta*, I, 616.

14 Bastien, *Directoire Canonique*, p. 230, n. 348.

15 Cf. *supra*, ch. II; Heston, "Some Aspects of Government in Religious Communities"—*The Jurist*, X (1950), 41-42; Schaefer, *De Religiosis*, p. 411, n. 187; Bastien, *Directoire Canonique*, p. 230, note 1; Battandier, *Guide Canonique*, n. 474; Creusen, *Religieux et Religieuses*, p. 127.

> Qu. 98: By what authority (Chapter, Council, General or Provincial Superior), on what principles and in what proportion are the contributions to the general and provincial funds determined?
> Qu. 99: Were these contributions paid willingly or more or less under pressure?
> Qu. 100: Are the Provinces and houses allowed to retain whatever is prudently foreseen to be necessary or very appropriate for their own life and growth in view of the good of souls and the welfare of the Institute?[16]

The fact that the superior general of the institute must state in his report to the Holy See the amount of surplus goods given yearly to the common treasury by the local houses and must explain whether these contributions were made freely and willingly seems to indicate that the legislator intends to safeguard these rights of local houses.

However, it must be borne in mind that, before computing the annual surplus of local houses, the local superior must deduct not only the operating expenses, the payments of interest of debts and the regular installments towards amortizement, but also the donations of the faithful given for the pursuance of the work particular to the local house.

> It should be borne in mind that the annual surplus is to be calculated on the basis of the balance of income over expenses, as accruing from ordinary operations. This point is very important nowadays, when religious institutes are, of necessity, expending so much time and effort to interest prospective benefactors with a view to endowment. Benefactors usually give their money to some phase of the institution's activity in which they have a special interest. This being the case, and in view of the scrupulous care with which canon 1514 demands that the intentions of the benefactors be honored, higher superiors may not require such benefactions to be included in the 'income' of a house or

---

[16] S.C. de Rel., 9 Dec. 1948—*AAS*, XL (1947), 378; cf. Bouscaren, *Canon Law Digest*, III, 175-176.

> province. Unless the contrary is explicitly stated, the will of the donor is to benefit a specific aspect of the institution's activity in the house which he favors, and it would derogate from his intention to draw off part of his donation, even for the benefit of the province . . .[17]

If, then, the benefactor explicitly states that his donation is given for the maintenance or furtherance of the work of a local house, the major superiors may not levy taxes on such goods. If the donor did not specify the purpose of his gift, and if particular law determines the destination of such gifts, the intention of the donor is presumed to be in conformity with the law. And in this case, the major superiors would be entitled to consider the donations as part of the taxable income of the house.[18]

### ARTICLE 4. MAJOR SUPERIORS AND THE RIGHT TO TRANSFER GOODS FROM ONE HOUSE TO ANOTHER

It is not within the domain of the major superior alone to administer directly and immediately each local religious house. This duty belongs to the local superior and to the official duly appointed according to the constitutions. Nevertheless, certain emergencies may warrant his intervention in a particular case.

In view of the property rights of local religious houses, the question arises as to whether the major superiors of the institute may, in special cases, transfer goods from one house to another, or from one province to another. May they freely dispose of the temporalities of local houses, or is the consent of local superior required to perform such transfer of property? Since the solution to this problem involves weighty practical consequences, it is necessary to examine every phase of general and particular law in order to arrive at a valid conclusion.

---

[17] Heston, *art. cit.* — *The Jurist*, X (1950), 43.

[18] ". . . nequit enim facere privatorum voluntas, ut quod a legitima potestate in bonum commune praecipitur certo destituatur effectu." Leo XIII, const. *Romanos Pontifices*, 8 May, 1881—*Fontes*, n. 582.

Before a solution can be reached, certain interpretation of the laws seem necessary. Canon 18 states clearly that ecclesiastical laws must be understood according to the proper meaning of the words found *in textu et contextu*. The first source of interpretation of laws, therefore, is the text and the context of the law itself. If, after close scrutiny, the full meaning of the law still remains doubtful, recourse may be had to other norms of interpretation, such as the meaning found in parallel passages in the Code, i.e. places where the Code treats of the same matter under other aspects; the purpose of the law; and the mind or intention of the legislator. If no legislation is found concerning a specific problem, a norm of action may be drawn from other sources: i.e., from laws enacted in similar matters, from the general principles of law, from the use and practice of the Roman Curia, and finally from the common and constant teaching of learned authorities..[19] With these concepts in mind, an attempt may now be made to solve the problem in relation to the superior general. The same principles may be applied *servatis servandis* to the provincial superior.

Two canons of the Code may be referred to, which treat, either explicitly or implicitly, of the powers of the superior general in the temporal administration of a local house.

> *The superior general has authority over all the provinces, and houses, and members of the institute, but he must exercise it as prescribed by the constitutions.*[20]
> *In every religious institute, all must carefully observe the common life, even in matters of food, clothing, and furniture.*[21]

The relation of the latter canon to the administrative powers of the superior general is only indirect. One might claim that the superior general, by virtue of canons 502 and 594, § 1 is empowered to transfer goods from one house to another, either to establish, or to maintain an equality of living standards in the different houses

19 Can. 20.

20 Can. 502.

21 Can. 594, § 1.

of the institute, where gross inequalities in income are found to exist. For example, the religious assigned to a parish which receives a large income may enjoy a standard of living much higher than the standard followed by the professors of a seminary. Therefore, to remedy such a situation, canon 594, § 1 might be invoked to justify the superior general in withdrawing money or goods from the parish income to subsidize the seminary.[22] However, the justifiability of these conclusions is doubtful, since such a practice is not mentioned in the law, and since other means are at the Superior's disposal to remedy such situations. As has been said previously in this chapter, according to the Normae of 1901,[23] taxes may be levied on local houses, according to the constitutions of each particular institute. It is therefore within the province of the superior general, with or without his council, according to the constitutions, to increase the tax levy on the houses with larger incomes or to lower the tax on the houses with smaller income, thus narrowing the income differential between the more and the less fortunately endowed houses. Therefore, if the annual taxes remedy this inequality, it seems superfluous to grant to the superior general the power of transfering goods from one house to another as an additional means of remedying this situation. Furthermore, the normal revenues of the general administration from the taxes should enable the superior general to subsidize or otherwise help the needy houses of the congregation. Although it might seem that the legislator should have granted broader powers to every superior general, it does not follow that the legislator did grant them. The law is based on what the legislator has said *de facto,* and not on what he should have said. If he proposed to grant such powers, this must appear from the text or context of the law. Otherwise, one may not say that such powers have been granted.

The other canon relevant to this problem states that the superior general of an institute has power over all provinces, houses and members of the institute, which power is to be exercised according

---

22 Huot, "La Doctrine Relative aux Biens Temporels"—*Acta et Documenta,* I, 629.

23 *Normae* of 1901, art. 294.

to the constitutions.[24] If the words of this canon are considered *in textu et contextu,* the Code does not grant to the superior general the power to effect transfers of temporal goods from one religious house to another. The power of the general over local houses is determined by the clause *exercendam secundum constitutiones.* Therefore, the common law of the Church does not settle this question, but leaves the last word in this matter to the particular law of each institute.

The constitutions of certain institutes explicitly grant to the superior general the power to transfer temporal goods from one local house to another. The constitutions of the Society of the Divine Word and of other institutes provide that the superior general may effect such transfers within the entire congregation.[25] However, the constitutions of a great number of institutes are silent on this matter. They neither deny nor grant this power to the superior general. Among these institutes, a distinction must be drawn between those that adhere to the centralized system of property and those that neither limit nor deny the right of property. The local houses of congregations that adhere to the system of centralization do not have the right of ownership. The congregation is the only moral person capable of ownership and is held responsible for the inferior moral persons of the congregation. The right granted to local houses by

---

[24] Canon 502.

[25] "Ideo Generalis, annuente Consilio generali, et Superior territorialis Consilio suo annuente, bona valet transferre in aliud, Superior autem territorialis ab una territorii domo in alia." *Constitutiones Societatis Verbi Divini,* arts, 604, 589; "Hinc Superior major, justa necessitatis causa postulante, jus habet, servatis juris nostri praescriptis, de persona in personam suae jurisdictionis bona illius propria transferendi . . . Salva sunto benefactorum voluntas, leges fundationis et jura quaesita." *Codex Juris Addititii Missionariorum Filiorum Imm. Cordis Mariae,* art. 188; "Pater Generalis de consensu suorum Assistentium et audito Administratoris generalis consilio, potest bona de Collegio ad Collegium transferre, cum id a totius Ordinis bono requiritur; attamen in translationibus caute omino procedendum est, ne jura quaesita et offerentium voluntate laedantur; audiendi igitur sunt Superior et consultores illius Collegii, cujus bona transferuntur." *Constitutiones Ordinis Matris Dei,* art. 334. These texts are taken from Gutierrez, art. cit.—*Acta et Documenta,* I, 558-559.

canon 531 is denied by the constitutions, and the property of such houses is part of the patrimony of the community. In such institutes, the superior general enjoys the right of transferring goods from one house to another. He may exercise this right without in any way violating the right of local houses. He is only administering the goods of the patrimony of the institute, which patrimony is totally subject to his powers of administration. Therefore, he violates the rights of no one and commits no injustice.

If the congregation does not adhere to the centralized system of property and if the constitutions are silent on this matter, it seems to the writer that the superior general of such institutes has no claim to this right. Canons 531 and 502, § 1, moreover, seem to confirm this opinion. Canon 531 grants to every religious house the right of ownership unless the constitutions limit or deny this right. Canon 502, § 1, on the other hand, declares that the superior general has power over all houses of the institute, *which power he must exercise according to the constitutions.* Therefore, if the constitutions do not limit nor deny the right of ownership of the local houses, and if they do not grant this power to the superior general, no transfer may be made by him. Since in such congregations canon 531 remains fully operative, a contrary practice would be in violation of the right of ownership of the local houses.[26]

Finally, canon 20 indicates the sources from which a norm of action should be drawn in the absence of a law, either general or particular, on a given problem. One of these sources is that taken from

---

[26] "Nam si quaelibet ecclesiastica persona juridica est verus proprietarius suorum bonorum, sequitur, ut nullus Superior major de illis bonis libere disponere valeat sine injustitia proprie dicta . . . Superior religionis major vel generalis nequit nec valide nec licite disponere de bonis alicujus monasterii vel conventus (seclusis statutis particularibus), nisi accedat liber consensus illorum qui legitimam monasterii administrationem habent."—Prummer, *Manuale Juris Caninici* (Friburgi-Brisgoviae: Herder, 1922), p. 419, n. 443; "In illis religionibus in quibus singulae domus habent jus proprietatis, Superior major aut generalis nequit sine aperta injustitia de bonis istarum domorum disponere. Potest quidem Superior major justas praestationes imponere, servatis servandis, sicut princeps civilis potest justa tributa imponere bonis privatorum, sed nihil aliud potest disponere de bonis istarum domorum."—Prummer, *op. cit.*, 256, n. 193.

laws enacted in similar matters. A religious institute may well be compared to a diocese, and the local houses likened to the individual parishes of a diocese. In its legislation concerning the temporal administration of dioceses and of parishes, the common law in no way grants the Ordinaries the right to make transfers of property from one parish to another. On the contrary, the rights of the Ordinaries in this matter are very limited. Canon 1519 states that the local Ordinary has the duty to *supervise* the administration of ecclesiastical goods within his diocese. It does not say that he has the right to *administer*. Hence, since canon 1495, § 2 grants all parishes the rights of ownership, of acquisition and of administration, and does not grant to local Ordinaries the right to limit or deny these rights, local Ordinaries may not transfer goods from one parish to another. This situation is closely analogous to that discussed above, and the laws applicable in the latter case seem also to apply to the problem concerning the right of the superior general to make transfers of property between local houses. Since the right of the superior general is one of supervision only, he may not transfer goods from one house to another unless the Supreme Pontiff has empowered him to do so.[27]

It might be objected, nevertheless, that where the right of ownership of local houses is not limited by the constitutions, the superior general could transfer property in virtue of the *jus eminens*. The *jus eminens* is generally understood to belong only to the public authority in a perfect society. In the Church, this *jus eminens,* at least in the full meaning of the term, is proper and exclusive to the Roman Pontiff as supreme head of the Church.[28] Superiors general cannot claim such a right unless the Supreme Pontiff has delegated it to them one way or another. Also, the *jus eminens* is generally understood to apply only in extraordinary cases when the common good requires the sacrifice of property on the part of inferior moral

---

[27] "In itself the law of the Code points to an arrangement that is somewhat parallel to that of parishes of a diocese in relation to the bishop. The parishes may be taxed, but their surplus funds cannot be taken by the bishop, each parish is a unit in itself. Deviations from this arrangement must be sanctioned by papal approval." O'Brien, *The Provincial Religious Superior,* p. 166.

[28] Cans. 1499, § 2, 1518.

persons. It is difficult to see how this right could apply within a religious congregation.[29]

Huot has proposed that even in the absence of a particular law limiting the right of property of the houses, the superior general has right to transfer property from a "wealthy" house to a "needy" one.[30] His argument is based on the social character of property. He maintains that since all property has a social character, *a fortiori* must it retain this character in religious congregations. Accordingly, he concludes that the property of a "wealthy" house should benefit the institute as a whole, and especially the needy houses. But in the absence of any determination by the constitutions, who is to determine when and how the property of wealthy houses should serve the needy ones? "Who but the superior general," asks Huot.[31] Therefore, the superior general has a right to transfer property from one house to another.

To substantiate his argument, Huot appeals to canons 20 and 1518. Canon 20 indicates the courses that should provide a norm of action in the absence of law on a given problem, one of which is a *lex lata in similibus.* Canon 1518 states that the Supreme Pontiff is the supreme administrator and dispensor of all ecclesiastical goods. This latter canon is considered by Huot as a *lex lata in similibus,* applicable to the present problem, and he argues thus: since the Sovereign Pontiff, by virtue of his supreme power over the entire Church, is able to transfer goods from one religious house to another, so, too, the superior general can do the same within his institute.

---

29 "Dominium altum cum sit quaedam applicatio jurisdictionis supremae Summi Pontificis, nulli Superiori ecclesiastico subalterno nec ulli Superiori religioso per se competit. Quapropter Superior religiosus quicumque, etiam generalis, nequit nec valide nec licite disponere de bonis alicujus particularis communitatis, nisi accedat consensus legitimus illorum qui communitatis administrationem detinent; vel nisi impetrata fuerit licentia apostolica; aut jus possidendi pro subalternis communtatibus, approbatis constitutionibus fuerit limitatum ac diminutum." Vromant, *De Bonis Ecclesiae Temporalibus,* p. 60, n. 50.

30 Huot, "La Doctrine Relative aux Biens Temporels"—*Acta et Documenta,* I, 624-633.

31 "A qui la compétence pour juger de la question? Pourquoi pas au Superieur Général?" Huot, *art. cit.*—*Acta et Documenta,* I, 629.

Secondly, Huot continues, canon 20 indicates, as another source of action, general principles of law applied according to canonical equity. Now, according to the natural law, property has a social function, and this is true, not only *a pari* but *a fortiori,* within a religious congregation. But the head of the institute is the only authority who is competent to implement this general principle. Therefore, the superior general may transfer property from one house to another whenever conditions justify the application of the general principle.

This opinion of Huot is certainly appealing to one's sense of Christian charity. Moreover, the arguments he uses are not to be discounted but nevertheless they seem far from convincing. The social character of property would justify some kind of regulation of private property by a government, such as levying taxes upon the wealthy, and using the money thus raised for the relief of the poor and needy. But it is not generally understood to justify a direct transfer by government authority of property from a wealthy person to a needy one. In a socially well-ordered state, the social character of property would be recognized by equitable social legislation and public institutions. Similarly, in a religious community this social character of property is recognized through taxation, a system of contributions generally sufficient to provide for the common good and the occasional relief of a needy house. Therefore, there does not seem to be a sufficient basis for the right of the superior general to transfer property directly from one house to another.

The appeal to canons 20 and 1518 does not seem justified, since the constitutions already provide a rule recognizing the social character of property. Even if it were justified, it would not lead to the conclusion that the superior general may directly transfer property from one house to another, simply because the constitutions are silent on this matter. It is argued that, since the Sovereign Pontiff has that power for the universal Church, the same powers should, therefore, be attributed to the superior general for his institute. But, the power of the Sovereign Pontiff is supreme and independent, by divine law, and cannot be limited by any positive law; whereas the power of the superior general, although supreme *secundum quid,* is not supreme in the absolute sense, as is that of the Sovereign Pontiff. The power of the superior general is not independent, but is strictly limited by the constitutions. His power over the goods of provinces and of houses is only mediate, i.e. must be exercised through inferior administrators.[32]

It would seem rash, therefore, to conclude that, since the Sovereign Pontiff could transfer goods from one religious house to another, this same right belongs to the superior general. According to canon 502, whatever power the superior general has (including whatever power he may have over temporal property, even considered according to its social character) must be exercised according to the constitutions. Moreover, since the argument appealing to the "general principles of law" is also based on the social character of property, it is open to the same objections.

### ARTICLE 5. RESPONSIBILITY OF MAJOR SUPERIORS FOR OBLIGATIONS INCURRED BY LOCAL HOUSES

Canon 536, § I states explicitly that each religious moral person is responsible for its debts and obligations. Therefore, as a general rule, each local house must answer for every onerous contract validly transacted by its administrators, and must not rely on the provincial or general funds to liquidate its debts and obligations. However, two exceptions to this rule may be established: 1) if the province or the community has obligated itself to liquidate the debts of the local house; 2) if a local house has been declared by particular law as incapable of juridical responsibility in temporal matters. In such cases, the religious superior, in granting the permission to incur debts, has been constituted the official representative of the province or of the community.[33]

---

32 Can. 502.

33 "McManus, *The Administration of Temporal Goods in Religious Institues,* p. 165: O'Brien, *The Provincial Religious Superior,* p. 178.

In the event that a local house, through its superior or treasurer, acts without the required permission of the major superiors in matters of extraordinary administration, the major superiors themselves are not held responsible for the obligations incurred by the contract. However, if the province or congregation benefits from such a transaction, the province or congregation would be responsible to the extent of that benefit.[34]

---

[34] Can. 536, § 4; Fanfani, *De Jure Religiosorum ad norman Codicis Juris Canonici* (2 ed., Taurini-Romae: Marietti, 1925), p. 176.

# CHAPTER VI

## THE LOCAL SUPERIOR AND AUTHORITIES OUTSIDE RELIGIOUS COMMUNITY

### ARTICLE 1. THE SOVEREIGN PONTIFF

The Sovereign Pontiff possesses over the temporal goods of religious houses certain rights which affect the power of local superiors, although in practice, the exercise of these rights is very limited. Canon 1518 declares that the Sovereign Pontiff is the supreme administrator and dispensor of all ecclesiastical goods.[1] Since the goods of religious houses are ecclesiastical, according to Canon Law,[2] it follows that the Sovereign Pontiff is the administrator of all religious patrimony. The Code states this principle without going into any detail. Consequently there are some pertinent questions to which the Code does not give the answer. Is the Sovereign Pontiff the owner of these goods? If he is not the owner, has he eminent domain over them and what is the nature and the limits of his power of administration?

Some pre-Code authors believed that religious goods were owned concomitantly by three persons: first, by God; then, by the Sovereign Pontiff; and finally by the community itself.[3] Bouix declared that the Roman Pontiff is the prime owner of *all* religious property and that the right of the community to its property is subordinate to that of the Pope.[4] In the letter *Cum Encyclicas,* Benedict XIV[5] seemed to favor the opinion that recognized him as owner as well as administrator of all ecclesiastical goods. *Est et illud etiam nobis perspectissimum communem esse canonistarum sententiam, Romanum Pontificem non distributorem sed dominum esse rerum Ecclesiae.* But, wishing to leave the question open to further discussion, he stated

---

1 Cf. Benedict XIV, epist. *Cum Encyclicas* 24 May, 1754 — Fontes, II, 428.

2 Can. 1497.

3 Tamburini, *De Jure Abbatus,* disp. XI, q. II, n. 4.

4 Bouis, *De Jure Regularium,* II, 273.

5 Benedict XIV, epist. *Cum Encyclicas,* 24 May, 1754 — *Fontes* II, 428.

a principle which is accepted by all: *At nos hujusmodi disputationem intactam volumus cum in praesentem id sufficiat Pontificem Supremum haberi dispensatorem; theologi quippe cum canonistis consentiunt, Papam quamvis etiam tantummodo in supremum distributorem agnoscatur posse utique ad mox expressas facti circumstantias de Ecclesiarum rebus libere decernere.*

It is an accepted principle today that the Sovereign Pontiff is not the owner of the goods of a religious house.[6] The dominium of the goods resides in the community inasmuch as it is a moral person subject to the laws of the Church and recognized by Her.

The second question, that of the right of eminent domain of the Sovereign Pontiff over religious property, is one to which the answer may have far-reaching consequences. To reach proper conclusions in this question, one must first define the term "eminent domain." According to Beste, eminent domain is the "legitimate power by which the supreme authority of a perfect society may, in certain circumstances, deprive inferior physical or moral persons of their goods for the common good of the entire body."[7] It will be seen, therefore, that this right of eminent domain does not imply the actual ownership of the property in question,[8] but rather an application of the primacy of the common good, according to which inferior moral persons must sacrifice their temporal goods if the welfare of the superior community requires such a course of action.[9]

---

[6] *Summa Theologica,* IIa-IIae, q. 100, art. I, ad 7um; Capello, *op. cit.,* II, p. 570, n. 602; Coronata, *Institutiones,* III, p. 119, n. 1197; Craisson, *Des Communautés Religieuses* (Paris: 1869), p. 385, n. 786; Beste, *Introductio in Codicem* (3 ed., Collegeville; St. John's Abbey, 1946), p. 742.

[7] Beste, *Introductio in Codicem,* p. 742.

[8] "Inde habetur in bona civium dominium eminens societatis civilis quod reapse non est dominii jus, sed auctoritas socialis, qua bona privata cum bono publico componuntur." — Lega, *Commentarius in Judicia Ecclesiastica* (3 vols., Rome: Libraria Cattolica, 1938), I, 369, note 2.

[9] Cappello, *Summa Juris Canonici in Usum Scholarum* (4 ed., 3 vols., Rome: Apud Aedes Univ. Gregor., 1945), II, 570, n. 602. "Summus Pontifex habet quidem *dominium altum* omnium bonorum ecclesiasticorum sicuti princeps civilis habet dominium altum omnium bonorum civilium, sed sicut princeps civilis nequit arbitrarie disponere de omnibus bonis ecclesiasticis. Potest quidem condonare bona ecclesiastica, quae in iniqua saecularizatione a laicis

The Pope may exercise this right whenever the necessity of the Church or the utility of the faithful requires such an action, since it is his duty to lead every religious to the attainment of the common good of the Church. Under these circumstances he may transfer goods from one religious house to another, condone spoliations or usurpations of religious property, and exact abdication of such goods. He may enact laws limiting the administrative activities of local superiors or officials, such as the laws found in the Code concerning the alienation of religious and ecclesiastical goods.[10] He may also reserve to himself certain acts of administration when he deems it necessary.[11] Conversely, and for the same reasons, he may even endow local superiors with faculties greater than those granted to them by the common law. In exercising his right of eminent domain, the Sovereign Pontiff must strive to follow the rules of equity, and compensate the religious houses for whatever damages may be caused. However, even in cases where he cannot compensate for the loss, he may exercise his power of eminent domain. In such cases, the individual so deprived may receive as compensation certain spiritual benefits from the treasury of the Church.[12]

In practice, it rarely happens that the Pope exercises his right of eminent domain. In some instances the Sovereign Pontiff has exercised this right by excusing from restitution the actual detainers of ecclesiastical property seized unlawfully.[13] Pius VII (1800-1823) exercised it after the French Revolution, when he declared that neither he nor his successors would pursue in justice the unlawful

---

usurpata fuerunt; potest concedere ecclesiam ordinis religiosi alii ordini, sed de his valent ea, quae princeps observare debet in sic dicta *expropriatione* bonorum privatorum; i.e. debet a) adesse gravis causa boni communis et b) concedi aequivalens compensatio."—Prummer, *Manuale Juris Canonici*, pp. 419-420, n. 443.

10 Beste, *Introductio in Codicem*, p. 742.

11 Wernz, *Jus Decretalium*, II, 173, n. 149.

12 Merkelbach, *Summa Theologiae Moralis* (3 vols., 8 ed., Montreal: Desclée, 1949), II, p. 342, n. 340.

13 Merkelbach, *Summa Theologiae Moralis*, II, p. 342, n. 340.

detainers of Church property which was alienated by the government during the Revolution.[14] A similar example is found in the Concordat between the Holy See and Italy.[15]

There remains to consider the third question, that of the nature and limits of the Pope's powers of administration. The administrative power of the Supreme Pontiff is supreme and complete (*plenum*); both mediate and immediate. *Immediate* administration means the direct management of ecclesiastical goods without any intermediaries. *Mediate* administration signifies the indirect management of property either through legislation or by intermediaries.[16] The Pope may posit all acts of administration that he deems necessary or useful; 1) to keep the property in good condition; 2) to make it productive; 3) to derive benefit from it; and 4) to apply, pay out and use it for legitimate purposes.[17] Acts performed in this connection need not be considered from the standpoint of whether they are ordinary or extraordinary in nature.

Since the Roman Pontiff is the head of such a vast organization, his personal management of all ecclesiastical property is impossible. Therefore, he exercises this power through the medium of the Sacred Congregations. Religious houses other than those in mission lands are administered through the Sacred Congregation of Religious.[18] Those in mission lands are subject to the Sacred Congregation of the Propagation of the Faith.[19]

In conclusion, it may be said that the Pope is the supreme administrator but not the owner of the goods of religious houses. The local

---

[14] Craisson, *op. cit.*, p. 385, n. 786.

[15] *AAS*, XXI (1929), 285; Bastien, *Directoire Canonique*, p. 225, note 2.

[16] Comyns, *Papal and Episcopal Administration of Church Property*, The Catholic University of American Canon Law Series, n. 147 (Washington, D. C.: The Catholic University of America Press, 1942), p. 60.

[17] Wernz, *Jus Deccretalium* III, n. 147; McManus, *The Administration of Temporal Goods in Religious Institutes*, p. 79; Larraona, "Commentarium Codicis"—*CpR*, XII (1921), 355-356.

[18] "Congregatio negotiis religiosorum sodalium praeposita ea sibi exclusive vindicat quae respiciunt regimen, disciplina studia, bona et privilegia religiosorum sodalium. . ." Can. 251.

[19] "Ejus jurisdictio iis est circumscripta regionibus, ubi sacra hierarchia nondum constitua, status missionis perseverat. . . " Can. 252, § 3.

religious house remains the owner of its goods. However, he may exercise his right of eminent domain, subject to the command of law, which dictates that the property rights of an inferior moral person are inviolable unless the common good of the Church requires that they be sacrificed.[20]

### ARTICLE 2. THE LOCAL ORDINARY

In order to complete this study of the temporal administration of religious houses pertaining to a non-exempt clerical pontifical institute, it is essential to know the extent of the rights of the local Ordinaries. The Code, in canon 1519, determines the extent of the administrative powers of the local Ordinary over temporal goods in general.

> § 1—*Loci Ordinarii est sedulo advigilare administrationi omnium bonorum ecclesiasticorum quae in territorio suo sint nec ex ejus jurisdictione fuerint subducta, salvis legitimis praescriptionibus, quae eidem potiora jura tribuunt.* § 2—*Habita ratione jurium, legitimarum consuetudinum et circumstantiarum, Ordinarii, opportune editis peculiaribus instructionibus intra fines juris communis, universum administrationis bonorum ecclesiasticorum negotium ordinandum curent.*

Certain pre-Code authors held the opinion that the jurisdiction of the Ordinary was analogous to that of the Sovereign Pontiff — as the Pope enjoyed supreme jurisdiction over the ecclesiastical goods of all moral persons in the Universal Church, so the Ordinary had jurisdiction over the ecclesiastical property of all moral persons in his diocese, except that of the exempt religious.[21] This opinion was still maintained even after the promulgation of the Code of Canon Law[22] but most modern commentators now agree that this analogy is not

---

20 Comyns, *op. cit.*, p. 164.

21 Werns, *Jus Decretalium,* III, nn. 15-51.

22 Blat, *De Rebus,* n. 434.

so close as was formerly held.[23] It is clearly stated in canon 1518 that the Sovereign Pontiff is the supreme administrator of all ecclesiastical property within the Church. He also has the right of immediate administration in the Universal Church; whereas the local Ordinary has the right of immediate administration over only those goods which belong to the diocese as a whole, or which have no other immediate administrator, v.g. the diocesan seminary, the cathedral church. The local Ordinary moreover has the right of vigilance over the administration of other ecclesiastical goods within his diocese which have their own immediate administrator, and which have not been withdrawn from his jurisdiction. Finally, the local Ordinary must supervise the administrators, to see that they accomplish their duties properly and faithfully in accordance with the law.[24] The Ordinary may also be said to be the mediate administrator of these same goods, in that he may and should enact particular instructions regulating the whole matter of the administration of ecclesiastical property within his diocese. In so doing, he may issue regulations not contained in the universal legislation of the Church, so long as these regulations are not contrary to the Code.[25]

Canon 618, § 2, 1° withdraws from the jurisdiction of the local Ordinary the property of the religious houses of a pontifical congregation, except in the cases mentioned in canons 533-535. In regard to these institutes, the local Ordinary may not make any change in the constitutions or inquire into the temporal administration, without prejudice to the dispositions of canons 533-535. The legislation of this canon has its source in the constitution *Conditae a Christo* where it is said that the administration of religious goods belongs to the superior general and that the bishop has no right to request any accounting of the administration.[26]

---

23 Claeys-Simenon, *Manuale Juris Canonici* (3 vols., Vol. I, 5 ed., Gnadae et Leodii: Prostat apud auctores in Seminariis Canavensi et Leociensi, 1939), I, n. 1006; Nebreda, "Quaestiones Selectae de Jure Administrativo Ecclesiastico"—*CpR,* VII (1926), 193.

24 Can. 1519, § 1.

25 Can. 1519, § 2.

26 " . . . bonorum quibus Sodalitia singula potiuntur, administratio penes Moderatorum supremus . . . esse debet. De iis nullam Episcopus rationem potest exigere." Leo XIII, const. *Conditae a Christo,* 8 Dec., 1900 — *Fontes,* n. 644.

The goods of religious houses of a pontifical institute subject to the jurisdiction of the Ordinary are mentioned in canons 533, § 1, 3°, 4° and in canon 535, § 3, 2°. In canon 533, § 1, 3°, it is stated that superiors of every religious house must obtain the previous consent of the local Ordinary to invest funds which have been donated or bequeathed to the house for expenditure in the locality on divine worship or on works of charity. The Ordinary also has jurisdicition over property given to a parish or a mission, or given the religious *intuitu paroeciae* (canon 533, § 1, 4°), since this property actually belongs to the parish and not to the institute. Before investing funds falling in these categories, therefore, the local superior should first obtain the permission of the local Ordinary, and, on request, render an accounting to him of such investments.

The legislation of canon 533, § 1, 3° is also found almost *verbatim* in the constitution *Conditae a Christo*.[27] The goods mentioned in canon 533, § 1, 3°, although belonging to a religious house, are the object of concern of the local Ordinary, since they are given for local purposes; i. e. for divine worship or pious works to be accomplished in the locality. The property mentioned in canon 533, § 1, 4° is that given to a parish or mission, or, if given the religious *intuitu paroeciae,* is presumed to be acquired by the parish or mission. These goods are not withdrawn from the jurisdiction of the local Ordinary since they belong to the parish and not to the institute. It is, therefore, reasonable that the local superior obtain the permission of the local Ordinary for the investments of such funds, and that the Ordinary be given the right to request an account concerning the administration of these funds.[28]

In considering further the prescriptions of this canon, two questions will be examined: (1) the nature of the investment, and (2) the nature of the goods involved in the investment.

The concept of investment has not been defined uniformly by canonists.[29] Yet, in spite of their differences in wording the defini-

---

27 *Conditae a Christo,* II, n. X, — *Fontes,* n. 644.
28 Can. 535, § 3, 2°.
29 Huot, *art. cit.* — *CpRM,* XXXIV (1955), 365.

tion, they agree in saying that it consists in the conversion of wealth or of resources from an unproductive form to a productive form.[30] Huot draws a distinction between an investment in the strict sense and in the broad sense. In its strict connotation, investment means a relatively permanent conversion of money into other goods, either movable or immovable, which will be preserved as stable capital and which will produce additional wealth. In its broader connotation, investment means to deposit money in a bank in order to protect it and receive interest.[31]

If the religious superior wishes to convert funds into another form of property, or income-yielding investments to be preserved as stable capital, the consent of the Ordinary is necessary. Whether this consent is necessary for validity or only for liceity has been the object of controversy among canonists. Larroana and Schaefer both admit that this act of administration is of an extraordinary nature, yet maintain that the consent of the Ordinary is necessary only for the liceity of the act.[32] Their opinion has been followed by McManus,[33] and is the more logical. As it has been said, the reason why the Code requires the Ordinary's permission for these investments is not because it is an act of extraordinary administration, but because of the concern that the Ordinary has for the security, productivity, and application of such funds.

In making restrictions on the local superior's freedom to invest funds donated or bequeathed to the house for local expenditure on divine worship or on works of charity, canon 533, § 1, 3° makes use of the word *fundus* to designate this class of property. It also makes use of the term to include other property, such as money or movable

---

[30] McManus, *The Administration of Temporal Goods in Religious Institutes,* p. 91; Larraona, "Commentarium Codicis" — *CpR,* XII (1931), 437; Quinn, *Relation of the Local Ordinary to Religious of Diocesan Approval,* The Catholic University of America Canon Law Studies, n. 283 (Washington, D. C.: The Catholic University of America Press, 1949), p. 108.

[31] Huot, *art. cit.* — *CpRM,* XXXIV (1955), 366.

[32] Larraona, "Commentarium Codicis" — *CpR,* XII (1931), 438-439; Schaefer, *De Religiosis,* p. 420, n. 196.

[33] McManus, *The Administration of Temporal Goods in Religious Institutes,* p. 93.

goods, but only in so far as it has been or will be converted into money, or into a form capable of being invested.[34] Ordinarily, however, this term is used to indicate only landed property, real estate, or real property.[35]

The religious house must come into possession of the property by an act of donation. The text of the canon (*tributi legative*) indicates that the donation must have been received either in the form *inter vivos* or *mortis causa.*

Pious foundations are defined as "property given in any way to any moral person in the Church with a burden that is perpetual or greatly protracted of devoting some of the annual income to the celebration of a certain number of masses, to the performance of other specified ecclesiastical functions, or to the carrying out of certain works of piety or charity."[36] Such foundations fall under Can. 533, § 1, 3°, if they fulfill the conditions mentioned in the canon. Pious foundations are not subject to this canon if they are established solely for the benefit of the religious without any relation to outside works of divine worship or charity; or if they consist of funds or legacies given to be spent immediately. Nor does the canon apply to other income of the house, such as salaries, stole fees, etc., or subsidies for the house from the Ordinary or from higher superiors.[37] This canon is applicable in cases where the will of the donor specifies that gift funds must be invested, and only the income be spent. This conclusion is obvious from the wording of canon 533, § 1, 3°, and from the source of this canon which indicates, as a reason for the supervision of the local Ordinary, the desire of the legislator to keep the property intact.[38]

---

[34] McManus, *op. cit.*, p. 103; Nebreda, *art. cit.*, — *CpR,* VII (1926), 114.

[35] Nebreda, *art. cit.* — *CpR,* VII (1926), 114; Vermeersch-Creusen, *Epitome,* I, n. 606, McManus, *op. cit.*, p. 102.

[36] Abbo-Hannon, *The Sacred Canons* (2 vols., St. Louis, Herder, 1957), II, 747. "Nomine piarum fundationum significantur bona temporalia alicui personae morali in ecclesiae quoquo modo data, cum onere in perpetuum vel in diuturnum tempus ex reditibus annuis aliquas missas celebrandi, vel alias praefinitas functiones ecclesiasticas explendi; aut nonnulla pietatis et caritatis opera peragendi." Can. 1544 § 1.

[37] Blat, *Commentarium* III, n. 258; Quinn, *op. cit.*, p. 108.

[38] Leo XIII, const. *Conditae a Christo,* II, n. IX — *Fontes,* n. 644.

Canon 533, § 1, 3° further states that the goods must be given to the *religious house itself*. By the word *domui* is understood the religious community, the moral person. Therefore, money given to the province or to the congregation does not fall within the scope of this canon, but may be administered solely by the provincial and the general superior, and may be invested in favor of a local house without the consent of the local Ordinary.[39] Certain authors take the opposite view — that if such funds, given to the province or to the institute are to be spent through a local house, their investment should be subject to the control of the Ordinary.[40] However, as Quinn says so well:

> The determining factor here is not alone a question of who will spend the funds, rather it must also be determined to whom the funds were given. Was it to the religious house or was it to the institute itself? The terminology of the canon together with the interpretation of the canonists restrict the case to funds given to the religious house . . . so that there seems no justification for extending its meaning.[41]

If a local house has no right to possess property; i.e., if its property belongs to the province or to the institute, any funds given to it do not fall under Canon 533, § 1, 3°. However, even if a parish is united *pleno jure* to the religious house, and if funds are given to the parish, the consent of the Ordinary is necessary to invest such funds.[42]

It must be said at this point that canon 533, § 1, 3° legislates only on funds and pious foundations given to the local religious house.[43] If the local house is united to a parish, and if such funds or pious foundations are given to the parish, they are subject to the legislation of canons 1544-1551; other funds are subject to canons 533,

---

[39] Quinn, *op. cit.*, p. 108; Blat, *Commentarium* III, n. 258.

[40] Farrell, *The Rights and Duties of the Local Ordinary Regarding Congregations of Women Religious of Pontifical Approval,* The Catholic University of America Canon Law Series, n. 128 (Washington, D. C.: The Catholic University of America Press, 1941), p. 147.

[41] Quinn, *op. cit.*, p. 110.

[42] C. 533, § 1, 4°.

[43] Larraona, "Commentarium Codicis" — *CpR,* XIII (1932), 29, note 544.

§ 1, 4° and 1536. Canon 1546, § I requires the consent of the local Ordinary only for pious foundations given to the *parish*, and not for those given to the *religious house*. Supplementary laws may be found elsewhere in the Code, but they can always be reconciled with those found in the last mentioned canons.

McManus gives cogent reasons for separating the legislation of pious foundations given to religious houses from the legislation concerning pious foundations given to parishes of religious.

> There is reason for separating the two for the fact that pious foundations established in churches will usually be concerned with Masses or church services, and over these the local ordinary has the right and duty of greater vigilance, unless they are established in churches of exempt religious. Moreover, the fact that a pious foundation has been established in a church rather than in a house of religious will often indicate that the donor wishes that the obligations be satisfied in that church (*eo ipso loco*) and not elsewhere. Hence, even though the religious depart from the locality, the church will in all probability remain, and the obligation attached to it will continue. In view of this possibility it can be seen that the local ordinary has a concern and an interest in the obligations assumed by the church and should, therefore, have corresponding powers. On the other hand, obligations assumed by the community go with the community wherever they go, and therefore, the power of the local ordinary over these need not be so extensive. This seems to be made clear by the canons on religious administration. Of these canons only the prescript of canon 533, § 1, 3° can apply to pious foundations. Now, according to that prescript the local ordinary has the right of supervision only when the foundation has been acquired by a *house* (not a province), and then only when the obligations are to be satisfied locally (*eo ipso loco*).[44]

[44] McManus, *The Administration of Temporal Goods in Religious Institutes*, p. 107.

The next condition to be fulfilled if the prescriptions of canon 533, § 1, 3° are to become operative is that the funds be given for use in the locality, *eo ipso loco.* Some authors contend that this clause refers not only to the city where the religious house is situated, but also to the entire diocese.[45] In their opinion, it would seem strange if the local Ordinary had the right to supervise the administration of property in one section of his diocese but not in another. The fact that should be ascertained is: "has the local Ordinary a right to supervise the administration of *this property?* If he has, he may exercise that right anywhere in his diocese."[46]

While granting that this opinion has some weight, based on the supposed intention of the legislator, one should consider that the words of the law offer strong reasons for the opposite. The more probable opinion seems to be that of Larraona who limits the place to the city in which the religious house is situated.[47] Larraona gives forceful arguments to prove his point. He readily admits that the term *locus* is sometimes used in the Code to designate the limits of the diocese; when, for example, the Ordinary of the place is mentioned.[48] But, basing his opinion on the context of canon 533, § 1, 3°, he concludes that the two modifiers *eo ipso* indirectly designate the location of the particular religious house whose superior is bound by the prescription. He also argues from the source of the canon, where there is explicit mention of that locality where the *certa domus* is situated.[49] This opinion seems to be more widely held among canonists.[50]

---

45 Vermeersch-Creusen, *Epitome,* I, n. 606; Nebreda, *art. cit.* — *CpR,* VII (1926), 323.

46 McManus, *op. cit.,* p. 109.

47 Larraona, "Commentarium Codicis" — *CpR,* XIII (1932) 34; Coronata, *Institutiones,* I, p. 680, note 9; Wernz-Vidal, *Jus Canonicum,* III, 181.

48 Can. 1516, § 3.

49 Leo XIII, const. *Conditae a Christo,* II, n. IX; "Qui vero fundi certae domui tributi legative sint a Dei cultum beneficientiamve *eo ipso loco* impendendam."

50 Coronata, *Institutiones,* I, p. 680, note 9: Wernz-Vidal, *Jus Canonicum* III, 181: "Uti apparet e contextu can. 533, § 1 ,n. 3, atque ex Constit. *"Conditae a Christo"* . . . "locus" intellegitur non dioecesis aut vicariatus seu praefectura apostolica, sed *pagum, oppidum seu civitas ubi certa domus est exstructa.* — Vromant, *De Bonis Ecclesiae Temporalibus,* p. 214, n. 4.

The final condition to be observed concerning the prescription of canon 533, § 1, 3°, as applied to religious houses of pontifical right, is the destination of the income accruing from the funds. The income must be destined to defray the expenses of divine worship or of local charities.[51] The income is set apart for divine worship if the funds were donated or bequeathed for offering of masses in the church of the religious, for the preservation or amelioration of the church, or for the purchase of new vestments.[52] The income will be destined for charitable purposes if the funds were given for the corporal works of mercy, for scholarships or for endowments. Spiritual works of mercy also come under this heading; namely, church services, catechising, care of orphanages or hospitals, teaching school, aid to the poor, etc. . . .[53] The obligation of obtaining the consent of the local Ordinary rests upon the local superior.[54]

Canon 533, § 1, 4° indicates another instance in which permission of the local Ordinary is required for the investment of money by religious administrators; namely, when the money has been given to a parish or mission administered by religious, or given to the religious for the benefit of a parish or mission.

This prescription is but a logical conclusion of canon 1536, § 1 where it is said: *"Nisi contrarium probetur, praesumendum ea quae donantur rectoribus ecclesiarum, etiam religiosorum, esse ecclesiae donata."* This doctrine dates back to the decree of Gratian[55] and the Decretals of Gregory IX,[56] and was later reaffirmed by Leo XIII.[57]

The Code defines a parish as a territory of a diocese with its own church, with a determined congregation having its proper pastor to provide for the care of souls.[58] By a *mission* is understood the entire

---

[51] " . . . ad Dei cultum beneficientiamve eo loco impendendam."

[52] Larraona, "Commentarium Codicis" — *CpR,* XIII (1932), 33; Quinn, *op. cit.,* p. 112; McManus, *op. cit.,* p. 104.

[53] McManus, *op. cit.,* p. 104.

[54] McManus, *op. cit.,* p. 111.

[55] c. 3, C. XII, p. 3.

[56] c. 15, X, *de testamentis et ultimis voluntatibus,* III, 26.

[57] Leo XIII, *"Romanos Pontifices",* 8 May 1881, — *Fontes,* n. 582.

[58] Can. 216, § 1.

territory of a vicariate or prefecture apostolic and not simply a limited part of the territory such as a quasi-parish.[59] It refers in general to those specific regions which are inhabited in great part by non-Catholics and pagan peoples, and which are under the care of religious institutes or societies of secular priests.

All non-exempt religious of pontifical approval are subject to this prescription. The subject of canon 533, § 1, 4° is ***religiosus quilibet,*** thus including all those concerned in canon 488, 7°.

The difficulty connected with this canon is that of determining whether the donations and gifts have been given to the religious themselves, or whether they have been given for the benefit of the parish or mission. In regard to formal donations and gifts, it is of prime importance that written proof of the intention of the donor concerning the purposes of the gift and the recipient of the gift be available.[60] Equally important is the obligation resting upon the religious administrators of such goods to make an inventory showing which belong to the religious community, and which to the parish or mission.[61] A separate account of both classes of goods should be carefully kept, so as to avoid misunderstandings between ecclesiastical and religious authorities.

Whenever the donor has not explicitly stated whether his donation was for the benefit of the religious or for that of the parish, the following rules should be applied to determine the nature of these offerings:

1. If the donor intends to bestow a benefit on the religious themselves, the gift is presumed to be acquired by the religious of the community; the rights of administration and of investment then belong to the superiors designated by the constitutions of the institute.

2. If the donor intends to bestow a gift to foster certain works of charity administered by a religious community, a distinction must be

---

[59] S.C. de Prop. Fide, ep. Easter 1922 — *AAS,* XIV (1922), 287-302; Leo XIII *const.* "Romanos Pontifices", 8 May, 1881, n. 14 — *Fontes,* n. 582.

[60] Larraona, "Commentarium Codicis"—*CpR,* XIII, (1932), 96, note 595.

[61] S.C. de Prop, Fide, 10 May, 1868 — *Fontes,* n. 582.

drawn to determine whether the work is under the control of the religious superior, or under that of the local Ordinary. If the benefit is bestowed on a project belonging to the religious, then the fund is owned by the religious, but its investment may be subject to the Ordinary according to canon 533, § 1, 3°, as explained above. On the other hand, if the fund is donated to a diocesan institution administered by religious, the fund belongs to the institution, and its investment is subject to the authority of the Ordinary, according to canon 1519.[62]

Leo XIII, in his constitution *Romanos Pontifices*[63] gave norms to be followed in this matter. He stated that the norms mentioned in the Second Council of Westminster are to be faithfully observed. The Council stated that one must first of all strive to discover the intention of the donor; but if this is impossible, his intention is to be interpreted according to the usual rules. These rules have been well summarized by Dailey.

> Monies received from the faithful by pew rent, the offertory collection, collections for the church or a part of it after sermons on special occasions and contributed by the parishioners of the same or of other parishes, collections from door to door, collections exacted by Sacred Congregation for the Propagation of the Faith or monies given by the wealthy at stated times are not gifts for the priest, but funds destined for his maintenance, *the fabrica,* the functions of divine worship and the payment of debts.[64]

---

62 Naz, *Traité de Droit Canonique,* I, 602; "Nulla ratio Ordinario loci danda est de fundis collatis primario intuitu *ipsorum religiosorum ita ut beneficentia maneat* proprie *personalis,* non *localis.*" — Vromant, *De Bonis Ecclesiae Temporalibus,* p. 216, n. 249.

63 Leo XIII, const. *Romanos Pontifices,* 8 May, 1881 — *Fontes* 582.

64 Dailey, *The Primary Effects of the Union Pleno Jure of Parishes with Religious Communities* (Rome; Catholic Book Agency, 1951), pp. 33-34. One of the reasons for the legislation of *Romanos Pontifices* is that there is a prevailing presumtion as to the intention of the donor. "In those places in which churches, being without goods, depend almost entirely upon the liberality of the faithful alone, donors are presumed to assure the proper execution of divine worship and the maintenance of religion in the manner prescribed

Despite the norms mentioned above, doubts may still arise as to whether the donor intended to give the money or the funds to the religious themselves, or to the parish or mission. To dispel such doubts, the following criteria may be followed. The administrator must always bear in mind the prescription of canon 1536, § 1: *Nisi contrarium probetur, praesumendum ea quae donantur rectoribus ecclesiarum, etiam religiosorum, esse ecclesiae donata.* This canon constitutes a presumption of law and to act against it requires real proof of the contrary. It is not, however, a presumption *juris et de jure,* since the supreme law in question is the will of the donor, and once this will is clearly known, it must be followed to the letter.[65]

Proof of the contrary may be gathered from the following considerations:

1. *The relation between the donor and the recipient.* This may indicate that the donor wishes to give to the person himself and not to the church, as for example, when a gift is given by a relative or by a close friend.[66]

2. *The circumstances accompanying the gift.* If the gift is given on the occasion of a personal service rendered by the religious, or on the occasion of an anniversary, one might conclude that the gift is personal.

3. *The nature of the gift.* If it consists of an object which is naturally destined for the personal use of the religious, v.g. clothes, a breviary, etc. A good indication will be the inscription of the recipient's name on the object.[67]

Religious houses of clerical institutes may be the recipients of mass foundations, and since such foundations are subject to special legis-

---

by authority. Therefore, when a law exists, which determines the times and causes of donations, the donors cannot always ad libitum determine the end for which the offerings are to be expended. They are presumed to wish to observe the law." Dailey, *op. cit.,* p. 34.

65 Vermeersch, *Periodica,* VI, suppl. XVII, 2.

66 Creusen, *Religieux et Religieuses,* n. 127, 4° ; Vermeersch, *Periodica,* VI, suppl. XVII, 40, sq.

67 Larraona, "Commentarium Codicis"—*CpR,* XIII (1932), 95.

lation it is proper to say a few words on the subject.[68] The prescriptions of the Code concerning mass foundations received by moral persons are found in canons 1545-1547. No mass foundation may be accepted without the previous permission of the local Ordinary. All non-exempt religious are subject to this prescription, which is necessary for the validity of the foundation.[69] The Code demands that the permission of the Ordinary be given in writing, but this written permission does not seem to be required for validity. This being the case, canon 11 may be applied, and an oral or a tacit permission appears sufficient for the validity of the foundation. A tacit permission seems to exist when the Ordinary is informed of the pious foundation and does not overtly oppose its acceptance.[70] It is also the duty of the Ordinary to determine the amount below which a pious foundation may not be established, as well as the norms for the proper distribution of the income.[71]

These prescriptions apply to all mass foundations given to religious, no matter whether a parish is united to the religious house or not. Even in cases in which the masses are to be said in a semi-public oratory of the religious house, the foundation remains subject to the vigilance of the Ordinary, and the formalities required by the Code of Canon Law must be fulfilled.[72]

A distinction must be made between mass foundations and mass stipends. The extent of the Ordinary's powers over the mass stipends received by non-exempt religious is determined by canon 843. It is evident from this canon that the mass stipends received by religious priests, *qua religiosi sacerdotes*,[73] are not covered therein, since they do not constitute a foundation. Only those stipends come under the vigilance of the Ordinary which have been received by religious who act as pastors or assistants in parishes, or who act as officials of other

---

[68] Can. 1544, § 1; Bouscaren-Ellis, *Canon Law, A Text and Commentary*, pp. 845-846.

[69] Can. 1546, § 1.

[70] Coronata, *Institutiones*, II, p. 510, note 5.

[71] Can. 1545.

[72] Cf. cans. 1544, 1545, 1546.

pious places. Therefore, stipends received by the superior of a clerical community, *quatenus communitati praesit,* are administered by the superior and not by the Ordinary.[74] If the stipends are received by religious priests assigned to a parish, the stipends are subject to the vigilance of the Ordinary, if the church is not a religious church. On the other hand, if they are assigned to a church belonging to the religious community, the stipends are subject only to the vigilance of the religious superior.[75]

---

[73] Vromant, *De Bonis Ecclesiae Temporalibus,* p. 217, n. 250.
[74] Vromant, *De Bonis Ecclesiae Temporalibus,* p. 217, n. 250.
[75] Can. 842.

## CONCLUSIONS

1. A formal decree of erection is not necessary for the establishment of a religious house. Whenever the legitimate religious superior and the proper authorities mutually cooperate to fulfill the conditions of law, all that is necessary is a manifestation, in some manner, of the will of the religious superiors to establish a religious house.

2. Every religious house is presumed to enjoy the right to property. The restriction or the limitation of this right must be proven and must accrue from a legitimate source.

3. The ultimate criterion to distinguish between acts of ordinary and of extraordinary administration of local religious houses lies in the object and in the mode of the particular administration. The *object* of administration comprises the maintenance, productivity and amelioration of property, including expenses necessary for the upkeep of persons according to their religious way of life. The *mode* of administrative acts is the manner in which such acts are performed, such as buying wholesale or retail.

4. The extent of ordinary administration of a religious house is determined by a preestablished and permanent order approved by competent authorities for each particular religious house. Extraordinary administration includes the administrative acts that go either beyond the object of ordinary administration or beyond the mode determined by the competent religious authorities for each particular religious house.

5. Unless the case be an exceptional one, superiors may not arbitrarily determine the ordinary or extraordinary nature of a specific act of administration.

6. By virtue of their mandate, the local superior and treasurer proceed validly without any explicit authorization in respect to acts of ordinary administration.

7. The local religious superiors of the United States must abide by the regulations of the Letter of the Apostolic Delegate to the United States of November 13, 1936, in regard to what is said concerning

the incurrence of debts, even though the interpretation of the general law of the Church on this matter as given by canonists is much broader.

8. In the performance of his administrative functions, the local treasurer is not autonomous, but is radically and completely subordinated to the authority and decisions of his local superior.

9. The local superior is never held personally responsible for damages caused by the local treasurer in the exercise of his function.

10. The major superiors of religious institutes that do not adhere to a system of centralized property may not transfer goods from one local house to another unless such a power has been granted to them by the constitutions or by immemorial or traditional custom in the institute.

11. Although the consent of the Ordinary, required in canon 533, § 1, 3°, 4°, concerns only the liceity of the act of administration involved, the act itself is one of extraordinary administration.

12. Pious foundations given to religious are subject to the prescriptions of canon 533, § 1, 3°, 4° provided they fulfill the conditions of the canon. They are not subject to this canon if they are established solely for the benefit of the religious without any relation to outside work of divine worship or charity.

13. Proof that a donation has been given to a religious assigned to a parish and not to the parish itself may be gathered from the relation between the donor and the recipient, the circumstances accompanying the gift and the nature of the gift.

## BIBLIOGRAPHY

### Sources

*Acta Apostolicae Sedis, Commentarium Officiale,* Romae, 1909-1929; Civitate Vaticana, 1929-

*Acta Sanctae Sedis,* 41 vols., Romae, 1865-1908.

Bouscaren, T. Lincoln, *The Canon Law Digest,* 4 vols., Milwaukee: The Bruce Publishing Co., 1934-1949-1953-1958.

*Bullarum Diplomatum et Privilegiorum Sanctorum Romanorum Pontificum Taurinensis Editio,* 24 vols., et Appendix, Augustae Taurinorium, 1857-1872.

*Codex Iuris Canonici Fontes,* cura Emi Petri Card. Gasparri editi, 9 vols., Romae (postea Civitate Vaticana): Typis Polyglottis Vaticanis, 1923-1939. (Vols. VII-IX ed. cura et studio Emi Iustiniani Card. Serédi).

*Codex Iuris Canonici Pii X Pontificis Maximi iussu digestus Benedicti Papae XV auctoritate promulgatus, Praefatione, Fontium Annotatione et Indice Analytico-Alphabetico ab Emo Petro Gasparri auctus,* Romae, Typis Polyglottis Vaticanis, 1917; reimpressio, 1948.

*Constitutions and Rules of the Congregation of the Missionary Oblates of the Most Holy and Immaculate Virgin Mary, The,* Rome: 1945.

*Corpus Juris Canonici,* editio Lipsiensis secunda, post Aemilii Ludovici Richteri curas instruxit Aemilius Friedberg, Lipsiae: 1879-1881; ed. anastatice repetita, 1955.

*Institutiones Ecclesiasticae Prosperi Lambertini . . .* postea Benedicti Decimi Quarti . . . Romae, Typis Sacrae Congregationis de Propagande Fide, 1747.

Jaffé, Philippe, *Regesta Pontificum Romanorum ab condita Ecclesia ad annum post Christum natum MCXCVIII,* 2 ed., correctam et auctam auspiciis Gulielmi Wattenbach, curaverunt L. Loewenfeld, F. Kaltenbrunner, P. Ewald, 2 vols. in 1, Lipsiae, 1885-1888.

Mansi, Joannes, *Sacrorum Conciliorum Nova et Amplissima Collectio,* 53 vols. in 60, Parisiis, Arnhem, Lipsiae, 1901-1927.

*Magnum Bullarium Romanum,* 18 vols., Luxemburgi, 1727.

Migne, J. P. *Patrologiae Cursus Completus, Series Latina.* 221 vols., Parisiis: 1844-1864.

*Monumenta Germaniae Historica, Gregorii I Papae Registrum Epistolarum,* edd. P. Ewald et L. Hartmann, Epistolarum Tomus I et II, Berolini, 1891-1899.

*Normae secundum quas S. Congr. Episcoporum et Regularium procedere solet in approbandis Novis Institutis Votorum Simplicium,* Typis S. C. de Propoganda Fide, 1901.

Schroeder, Henry J., *Canons and Decrees of the Council of Trent,* Original Text with English Translation, St. Louis: Herder, 1941.

### Reference Works

Abbo, John—Hannan, Jerome, *The Sacred Canons,* 2 vols., St. Louis: Herder, 1957.

*Acta et Documenta Congressus de Statibus Perfectionis,* 4 vols., Romae, Pia Societa San Paolo, 1950.

Augustine, Charles, *A Commentary of the New Code of Canon Law,* 8 vols., Vol. II, 4 ed., 1923; Vol. III, 5 ed., 1938; Vol. IV, 2 ed., 1921; Vol. VI, 2 ed., 1923; Vol. VIII, 1922, St. Louis: Herder.

Bastien, Pierre, *Directoire Canonique à l'Usage des Congrégations à Voeux Simples,* 5 ed., Bruges, Beyaert, 1951.

Battandier, Albert, *Guide Canonique pour les Constitutions des Instituts à Voeux Simples,* 6 ed., Paris: 1923.

Besson, Jules, *L'Instruction "Inter Ea",* Paris: Beauchesne, 1912.

Beste, Udalricus, *Introductio in Codicem,* 3 ed., Collegeville, Minn.: St. John's Abbey Press, 1946.

Blat, Albertus, *Commentarium Textus Codicis Juris Canonici,* 5 vols., in 6, Lib. II, *Jus de Religiosis,* 3 ed., Romae: "Apud Angelicum", 1938.

Bouix, Dominicus, *Tractatus de Jure Regularium,* 3 ed., 2 vols., Parisiis, 1883.

Bouscaren, T. Lincoln—Ellis, Adam, *Canon Law, a Text and Commentary,* 2 ed., Milwaukee; The Bruce Publishing Co., 1951.

Brisebois, Guy Marie, *De Natura Juridica Domus Religiosae,* Romae, Pontificium Athenaeum Antonianum, 1953.

Brown, Brendon, *The Canonical Juristic Personality with Special Reference to its Status in the United States of America,* The Catholic University of America Canon Law Series, n. 39, Washington, D. C.: The Catholic University of America, 1927.

Butler, Cuthbert, *The Lausiac History of Palladius,* 2 vols., Cambridge, 1898.

Cappello, Felix, *De Censuris juxta Codicem Juris Canonici,* Augustae Taurinorum, Marietti, 1919.

———, ———, *Summa Juris Canonici in Usum Scholarum,* 4 ed., 3 vols., Rome: Apud Aedes Universitatis Gregorianae, 1945.

Carlo, Camillus De, *Jus Religiosorum,* Parisiis, Desclée, 1950.

Cerato, Prosdocimus, *Censurae Vigentes ipso facto a Codice juris canonici excerptae cum suspensionibus ferendae sensentiae, poenis vindicativis, remediis poenalibus, poenitentiis et irregularitatibus,* 2 ed., recognita, Pativii, Typis Seminarii, 1921.

Claeys Bouuaert, F.—Simenon, G., *Manuale Juris Canonici,* 3 vols., Vol. I, 5 ed., Gnadae et Leodii: Prostat apud auctores in Seminariis Gandavensi et Leodiensi, 1939.

Clancy, Joseph, *The Local Religious Superior,* The Catholic University of America Canon Law Series, n. 175, Washington, D. C.: The Catholic University of America, 1943.

Cleary, Joseph, *Canonical Limitations on the Alienation of Church Property,* The Catholic University of America Canon Law Series, n. 199, Washington, D. C.: The Catholic University of America, 1936.

Comyns, Joseph, *Papal and Episcopal Administration of Church Property,* The Catholic University of American Canon Law Series, n. 147, Washington, D. C.: The Catholic University of America, 1942.

Coronata, Matthaeus Conte a, *Institutiones Juris Canonici,* 5 vols., Vol. I, 4 ed., 1949; Vol. II, 4 ed., 1951; Vol. III, 3 ed., 1948; Vol. IV, 3 ed., 1948; Vol. V, 3 ed., 1951, Taurini-Romae: Marietti.

Craisson, D., *Des Communautés Religieuses à Voeux Simples,* Paris: Librairie Poussielgue, 1869.

Creusen, Joseph, *De Juridica Status Religiosi Evolutione,* Romae: Apud Aedes Pontificiae Universitatis Gregorianae, 1948.

————, ———, *Religieux et Religieuses d'après le Droit Ecclésiastique,* 6 ed., Paris: Desclée de Brower, 1950.

————, ———, *Religious Men and Women in the Code,* translated by Edward Garesché, 3 Eng. ed., by Adam Ellis, Milwaukee: The Bruce Publishing Co., 1940.

Dailey, Robert, *The Primary Effects of the Union Pleno Jure of Parishes with Religious Communities,* Rome: The Catholic Book Agency, 1951.

Doheny, William, *Church Property, Modes of Acquisition,* The Catholic University of America Canon Law Series, n. 41, Washington, D. C.: The Catholic University of America, 1927.

————, ———, *Practical Problems in Church Finance,* Milwaukee: The Bruce Publishing Co., 1941.

Fagnanus, Prosper, *Commentaria in Quinque Libros Decretalium,* 5 vols. in 3, Coloniae Allobragum: 1759.

Fanfani, Ludovicus, *De Jure Religiosorum* 3 ed., Rovigo: Instituto Padano di Arti Graphice, 1949.

Farrell, Benjamin, *The Rights and Duties of the Local Ordinary Regarding Congregations of Women Religious of Pontifical Approval,* The Catholic University of America Canon Law Series, n. 128, Washington, D. C.: The Catholic University of America, 1941.

Ferraris, Lucius, *Prompta Bibliotheca Canonica Juridica, Moralis, Theologica, necnon Ascetica, Polemica, Rubricistica, Historica,* 9 vols., Rome: 1885-1892.

Flanagan, Bernard, *Canonical Erection of a Religious House,* The Catholic University of America Canon Law Studies, n. 179, Washington, D. C.: The Catholic University of America, 1943.

Fournier, Edouard, *Nouvelles Recherches sur les Curies, Chapitres, et Universités de l'Ancienne France,* Paris, Edouard Fournier, 1942.

Génicot, Edouard, *Theologiae Moralis Institutiones* quae in Collegio Lovaniensi Societatis Jesu tradebat Eduardus Genicot., 6 ed., quam recognovit I. Salsmans, Bruxelles: A Lewitt, 1909.

Goyneche, S., *Quaestiones Canonicae de Jure Religiosorum,* 2 vols., Neapoli: D'Auria, 1954.

Guyot, Joseph-Nicolas, *Répertoire Universel et Raisonné de Jurisprudence Civile, Criminelle, Canonique, et Bénéficiale,* 17 vols., Paris; Visse, 1784-1785.

Héfélé, Carolus—Leclercq, Henricus, *Histoire des Conciles,* 10 vols. in 19, Paris: Letouzey et Ané, 1907-1952.

Heston, Edward, *The Alienation of Church Property in the United States,* The Catholic University of America Canon Law Studies, n. 132, Washington, D. C.: The Catholic University of America, 1941.

Holbock, Carolus, *Tractatus de Jurisprudentia Sacrae Romanae Rotae,* Graetiae-Vindobonae-Coloniae: In Officina Libraria "Styria," 1957.

Kindt, Gerardus, *De Potestate Dominativa in Religione,* Universitas Catholica Louvaniensis Dissertationes, Series II, Tomus 34, Brugis-Parisiis-Romae: Desclée de Brower, 1945.

Kurtcheid, Bertrandus, *Historia Juris Canonici, Historia Institutorum,* Romae: Officium Libri Catholici, 1951.

Larraona, Arcadius, *Schema Lectionum circa Jura Patrimonilia,* Romae: Universitas Lateranensis, 1937.

Leage, R. W., *Roman Private Law,* 2 ed., by C. H. Ziegler, London: Macmillan, 1951.

Lega, Michaelis, *Commentarius in Judicia Ecclesiastica juxta Codicem juris canonici,* auctore Mich. Card. Lega; curante Victorio Bartocetti . . ., 3 vols., Rome: Anonima Libraria Cattolica Italiana, 1938.

Lesne, Emile, *Histoire de la Propriété Ecclésiastique en France,* 6 vols., Lille: Faculté Catholique, 1910-1943.

Leuren, Peter, *Forum Beneficiale,* Venetiis, apud Jo. Baptistam Recurti, 1742.

Merkelbach, Benedictus, *Summa Theologiae Moralis ad mentem D. Thomae et ad Norman Juris Novi,* 3 vols., 8 ed., Montréal: Desclée, 1949.

Michiels, Gommarus, *Principia Generalia de Personis in Ecclesia,* Lublin, 1932.

McGrath, Robert, *The Local Superior in Non-Exempt Clerical Congregations,* The Catholic University of America Canon Law Series, n. 351, Washington, D. C.: The Catholic University of America, 1954.

McLaughlin, Terence P., *Le Très Ancien Droit Monastique de l'Occident* Paris: Picard, 1935.

McManus, James, *The Administration of Temporal Goods in Religious Institutes,* The Catholic University of America Canon Law Series, n. 109, Washington, D. C.: The Catholic University of America, 1937.

Mocchegiani, Petrus, *Jurisprudentia Ecclesiastica,* 3 vols., Rome: 1904.

Naz, Raoul, *Traité de Droit Canonique,* 4 vols., 2 ed., Paris: Letouzey et Ané, 1955.

Noldin, Hieronymus, *De Censuris,* Oeniponte Lipsiae: F. Rauch, 1940.

O'Brien, Romaeus, *The Provincial Religious Superior,* The Catholic University of America Canon Law Studies, n. 258, Washington, D. C.: The Catholic University of America, 1947.

Ottaviani, Alaphridus, *Institutiones Juris Publici Ecclesiastici,* Romae: Apud Aedes Facultatis Juridicae S. Apollinaris, 1912.

Pejska, Josephus, *Jus Canonicum Religiosorum,* 3 ed., Friburgi, Brisgoviae: Herder, 1927.

Pharr, Clyde, *The Theodosian Code,* Princeton: The Princeton University Press, 1952.

Prummer, Dominicus, *Manuale Juris Canonici,* Friburgi, Brisgoviae: Herder: 1922.

Quinn, Stephen, *Relations of the Local Ordinary to Religious of Diocesan Approval,* The Catholic University of America Canon Law Series, n. 283, Washington, D. C.: The Catholic University of America, 1949.

Redoano, Guglielmo, *De Rebus Ecclesiae non Alienandis,* Placentiae: 1589.

Regatillo, Eduardus, *Institutiones Juris Canonici,* 2 vols., 4 ed., Santander: "Sal Terrae", 1951.

———, ———, *Interpretatio et Jurisprudentia Codicis Juris Canonici,* 3 ed., Santander: "Sal Terrae", 1953.

Reiffenstuel, Anacletus, *Jus Canonicum Universum,* 5 vols., Antwerp: 1743.

*Sanctae Romanae Rotae Decisiones seu Sententiae quae . . . prodierunt anno 1912 . . .,* Romae, Typis Vaticanis, 1912——.

Schaefer, Timotheus, *De Religiosis ad Norman Codicis Juris Canonici,* 3 ed., Romae: S.A.L.E.R., 1940.

Schmalzgruber, Franciscus, *Jus Ecclesiasticum Universum,* 5 vols. in 12, Romae: 1843-1845.

Sipos, Stephanus, *Enchiridion Juris Canonici,* 6 ed., Romae: Herder, 1954.

Sirmond, Jacobus, *Concilia Antiqua Galliae,* 3 vols., Paris: 1621.

Sotillo, Laurentius, *Compendium Juris Publici Ecclesiastici,* 2 ed., Santander: "Sal Terrae", 1951.

Stenger, Joseph, *The Mortgaging of Church Property,* The Catholic University of America Canon Law Series, n. 169, Washington, D. C.: The Catholic University of America, 1942.

Suarez, Franciscus, *Opera Omnia,* ed. nova, 28 vols., Tom. I-IV a D.M. Andre; Tom. V-XXVI a Carolo Berton, Parisiis, 1856-1878.

Tamburini, Ascanio, *De Jure Abbatum et Aliorum Praelatorum,* 4 vols., Coloniae Agrippinae: 1691.

Van Espen, Zegerus Bernardus, *Jus Ecclesiasticum Universum,* 5 vols., Louvain: 1778.

Vermeersch, A., *De Religiosis Institutis et Personis Tractatus Canonico-Moralis ad Recentissimas Leges Exactus,* 2 vols., Brugis, 1902-1904.

Vermeersch, A.—Creusen, J., *Epitome Juris Canonici cum Commentariis ad Scholas et ad Usum Privatum,* 3 vols., Vol. I, 3 ed., 1927; Vol. II, 2 ed., 1925; Vol. III, 2 ed., 1925, Mechlinae-Romae: Dessain.

Vromant, G., *De Bonis Ecclesiae Temporalibus,* 3 ed., Bruges-Paris: Desclée de Brower, 1953.

Wernz, Franciscus X., *Jus Decretalium ad usum Praelectionum in Scholis Textus Canonici sive Juris Decretalium,* 2 ed., 6 vols., Romae-Prati, 1899-1913.

Wernz, F.—Vidal, Petrus, *Jus Canonicum ad Codicis Norman Exactum,* 7 toms. in 8 vols., Romae: Apud Aedes Universitatis Gregorianae, 1923-1938; Tom. II, *De Personis,* 2 ed., 1928; Tom. III *De Religiosis,* 1933; Tom. IV, Pars I-II, *De Rebus,* 1934-1935.

Zeiger, Ivo A., *Historia Juris Canonici,* 2 vols., Romae: Apud Aedes Universitatis Gregorianae, 1939.

## ARTICLES

Capello, Felix, "Annotationes" — *Periodica,* XVIII (1929), 256-259.

Couly, A., "Administration" — *Dictionnaire de Droit Canonique,* I, 192-214.

Creusen, Josephus, "Fondation des Maisons Religieuses" — *Revue des Communautés Religieuses,* XI (1935), 63-69, 97-104, 122-131.

De Witt, George, "The Alienation of Church Property" — *The Jurist,* XIV (1954), 394-409.

Ellis, Adam, "Triginta Millia Libellarum seu Francorum" — *Periodica,* XXVII (1938), 348-353.

Gutierrez, Anastasius, "Quaestiones Canonicae circa Bona Ecclesiastica" — *Acta et Documenta Congressus Generalis de Statibus Perfectionis,* I, 554-604.

Heston, Edward, "De Notione Juridica Capitalis Stabilis" — *Acta et Documenta Congressus Generalis de Statibus Perfectionis,* I, 618-623.

———, ———, "Some Aspects of Government in Religious Communities"— *The Jurist,* X (1950), 34-51.

———, ———, "The Element of Stable Capital in Temporal Administration" — *The Jurist,* II (1942), 120-133.

Huot, Dorius, "Bonorum Temporalium apud Religiosos Administratio Ordinaria et Extraordinaria" — *CpRM,* XXXIII (1954), 60-76, 312-328; XXXIV (1955), 55-64, 175-192, 266-273, 364-373.

Janssens, J., "Aliénation des Biens Ecclésiastiques" — *Revue des Communautés Religieuses,* (1927), 118-120, 150-155, 164-168.

Laprat, R., "Commendes" — *Dictionnaire de Droit Canonique,* III, 1029-1085.

Larraona, Arcadius, "Commentarium Codicis" — *CpR,* III (1922), 45-53; XIII (1932), 24-35, 92-97, 184-195, 353-362;

XIV (1933), 38-44, 169-182, 252-256, 345-355, 416-425.

XV (1934), 18-23, 110-114, 204-208, 262-271.

Maroto, Philippus, "Annotationes" — *CpR,* X (1929), 341-343.

Nebreda, Eulogius, "Quaestiones Selectae de Jure Administrativo Ecclesiastico" — *CpR,* VII (1926), 107-118, 191-198, 261-271, 317-333.

Reed, I., "Triginta Millia Libellarum seu Francorum" — *Periodica,* XXXVI (1947), 213-230.

Vermeersch, Arthurus, "Annotationes" — *Periodica,* X (1921), 34-35.

——— "Aliénations des Biens Ecclésiastiques" — *Le Canoniste Contemporain,* X (1888), 335-350.

PERIODICALS

*Commentarium pro Religiosis,* Romae, 1920——; ab anno 1935: *Commentarium pro Religiosis et Missionariis.*

*Jurist, The,* Washington, D. C., 1941——.

*Le Canoniste Contemporain,* Paris, Lethielleux, 1878-1926.

*Revue des Communautés Religieuses,* Enghien, Belgique, 1925——.

*Periodica de Religiosis et Missionariis,* Brugis, 1905-1919; ab anno 1920: *Periodica de Re Canonica et Morali, utilia praesertim Religiosis et Missionariis,* Brugis, 1920-1927; ab anno 1927: *Periodica de Re Morali, Canonica, Liturgica,* Brugis, 1927-1936, et Romae, 1937——.

UNPUBLISHED THESIS

Carew, W. A., *The Apostolic Delegate,* University of Ottawa Canon Law Series, n. 32, Ottawa, Ontario: The University of Ottawa, 1950.

ABBREVIATIONS

*AAS* — *Acta Apostolicae Sedis*

*Acta et Documenta* — *Acta et Documenta Congressus Generalis de Statibus Perfectionis*

*Bull. Rom. Taur.* — *Bullarum Diplomatum et Privilegiorum Romanorum Taurinensis Editio*

*CpR* — *Commentarium pro Religiosis*

*CpRM* — *Commentarium pro Religiosis et Missionariis*

*DDC* — *Dictionnaire de Droit Canonique*

*Fontes* — *Codicis Juris Canonici Fontes cura . . .* Gasparri editi

Jaffé — *Regesta Pontificium Romanorum*

Mansi — *Sacrorum Conciliorum Nova et Amplissima Collectio*

*MGH* — *Monumenta Germaniae Historica*

*MPL* — Migne, *Patrologiae Cursus Completus, Series Latina*

*Periodica* — *Periodica de Re Canonica et Morali utili praesertim Religiosis et Missionariis*

*RCR* — *Revue des Communautés Religieuses*

S.C. Consist. — Sacra Congregatio Consistorialis

S.C. de Prop. Fide — Sacra Congregatio de Propaganda Fide

S.C. de Rel. — Sacra Congregatio de Religiosis

# ALPHABETICAL INDEX

## BIOGRAPHICAL NOTE

Francis L. Demers, O.M.I. was born on September 6, 1928, in Manchester, New Hampshire. At the completion of his elementary education at St. Anthony's parochial school, he attended the Manchester Central High School for two years. In 1944, he entered the Oblate Seminary at Bucksport, Maine, where he completed his high school studies. He received the first two years of his college education at the Oblate Seminary of Bar Harbor, Maine. He then entered the novitiate of the Oblates of Mary Immaculate at Colebrook, New Hampshire, where he made his religious profession on August 2, 1949. After completing his college and theological training at the Oblate College and Seminary, Natick, Massachusetts, he was ordained to the priesthood at the Sacred Heart Church of South Natick, Massachusetts, on June 17, 1955. In the fall of the same year, he entered the School of Canon Law of the University of Ottawa, Ontario, Canada, and received the degree of Bachelor of Canon Law in June, 1956, and the Licentiate of Canon Law in June, 1957.

## CANON LAW STUDIES*

392. Adams, Rev. Donald E., A.B., J.C.L., The Truth required in the *preces* for rescripts.
393. Bégin, Rev. Raymond F., A.B., S.T.L., J.C.L., Natural law and positive law.
394. Clancy, Rev. Walter B., A.B., J.C.L., The rites and ceremonies of sacred ordination.
395. Cox, Rev. Ronald J., S.T.L., J.C.L., A study of the juridic status of laymen in the writing of the medieval canonists.
396. Demers, Rev. Francis L., O.M.I., A.B., J.C.L., Temporal administration of the religious house in a non-exempt clerical pontifical institute.
397. Dziadosz, Rev. Henry J., M.A., S.T.L., J.C.L., The provisions of the Decree "Spiritus Sancti munera": the law for the extraordinary minister of confirmation.
398. Gerhardt, Rev. Bernard C., A.B., S.T.L., J.C.L., Interpretation of rescripts.
399. Hackett, Rev. John H., A.B., J.C.L., The concept of public order.
400. Murphy, Rev. Richard J., O.M.I., S.T.L., J.C.L., The canonico-juridical status of a communist.
401. O'Connor, Rev. David, M.S.SS.T., J.C.L., Parochial relations and cooperation of the religious and secular clergy.

*For a complete list of the available numbers of this series apply to the Catholic University of America Press, 620 Michigan Avenue, N.E., Washington (17), D. C., for a general catalogue.

www.ingramcontent.com/pod-product-compliance
Lightning Source LLC
LaVergne TN
LVHW050221080826
844660LV00012B/446

* 9 7 8 0 8 1 3 2 2 5 5 6 2 *